the
Effective
Director

the
Effective
Director

the essential guide to director
& board development

Edited by Chris Pierce

AMED
the developer's network

KOGAN
PAGE

First published in 2001 by Kogan Page Limited
Reprinted in 2001

Kogan Page Limited
120 Pentonville Road
London N1 9JN
UK

© AMED, 2001

This book has been endorsed by the Institute of Directors.

The endorsement is given to selected Kogan Page books which the IoD recognizes as being of specific interest to its members and providing them with up-to-date, informative and practical resources for creating business success. Kogan Page books endorsed by the IoD represent the most authoritative guidance available on a wide range of subjects including management, finance, marketing, training and HR.

The views expressed in this book are those of the authors and are not necessarily the same as those of the Institute of Directors.

British Library Cataloguing in Publication Data

A CIP record for this book is available from the British Library.

ISBN 0 7494 3551 8

Typeset by JS Typesetting, Wellingborough, Northants
Printed and bound in Great Britain by Creative Print and Design (Wales) Ebbw Vale

Contents

List of contributors

AUTHORS

Stephen Cowburn has spent his working life in a variety of human resource and management development roles in the telecommunications industry and latterly in professional services firms. His interest in director development comes from two directions. One is his observations of the effects of delayering management levels within an organization and the ways in which the board then visibly defines, communicates and champions its response to change. The second is his work with senior managers to enable them to develop into director roles. He holds an MBA from Cranfield University and is a fellow of the Chartered Institute of Personnel and Development.

Bob Garratt is a board and director development consultant in London and chairman of Organisation Development in Hong Kong and Media Projects International in London. He has an international practice in director development and strategic thinking. He is a member of the Professional Standards Committee and Chartered Accreditation Board Committee of the Institute of Directors, London; he is a past chairman of the Association for Management Education and Development and a member of the Guild of Management Consultants. He is a visiting professor of the Management School within Imperial College of Science Technology and Medicine at London University, and senior associate of the Judge Institute of Management, Cambridge University. His books include: *The Learning Organisation: Developing democracy at work* (2000), *Twelve Organisational Capabilities: Valuing people at work* (2000), *The Fish Rots from the Head: The crisis in our boardrooms* (1996), *Developing Strategic Thought: Rediscovering the art of direction giving* (1995), *Learning to Lead* (1991), *The Learning Organisation* (1987), *China Business Briefing*, with Sally Garratt, 'Breaking down barriers, priorities and practice', in *International Management Education* (1980), with John Stopford.

Julia Green is a psychoanalyst (a member of the Centre for Freudian Analysis and Research, London) and organizational psychologist who works with individuals and organizations on issues of change. She holds a master's degree in organizational psychology and is a chartered psychologist. She has been an active member of AMED for many years and is a past Council member. Julia has also served as a school governor and chair of the board of governors, and as a charity trustee and vice-chair of the management committee. Her current practice includes director development issues both in the not-for-profit sector and in the international information technology and manufacturing industries.

Keith Griffiths was the group training director for Flemings investment bank. Keith is a governor of the Examinations Board of the Securities Institute and a member of the Financial Services Authority Training Advisory Panel. He has been actively involved in director development both nationally and internationally. He has led formal courses and been responsible for director programmes involving coaching, mentoring and structural succession planning. Keith is now a consultant working primarily in the financial services industry.

Jennie Kettlewell's career spans both advertising and public relations. She was appointed to her first company directorship in 1989 and first managing director role in 1994. In 1995, she was invited to become chief executive of Shandwick Communications Ltd, a subsidiary of Shandwick plc, the world's largest PR consultancy. Jennie joined Bulletin International in 1998 as a director, with operational management responsibility for its six companies round the world. Her director development included the diploma in company direction from the

Institute of Directors, where she is a member. In her director role she became interested in the effect of harnessing the real potential of staff. This interest has led to her new role as a management development consultant and business performance coach. Jennie is on the Interviewer Panel for the IoD chartered director programme.

Paul Knutson is the principal of System Sense Ltd, an independent consultancy established in 1986 to assist companies with significant change, strategy formulation and planning, major cost reduction, management of complex projects and development of management teams. Clients have included market leaders in financial services, manufacturing, travel, the NHS, health sciences, electronic publishing and a software house. He has been responsible for systems for both Thomson Holidays and Amersham International. Paul has been an active member of AMED for many years.

Chris Pierce is a professional standards executive at the Institute of Directors in Pall Mall, London. His consultancy work has included clients in Europe, Africa, the Middle East and South East Asia. He has been teaching executive groups in the UK and overseas for over 20 years and has held senior management positions in the Overseas Development Administration, British Airways and Leeds Business School. He has written extensively on director and board development issues. His publications include: *Directing your Business*, volumes 1 and 2 (1997), *Developing your Business*, volumes 1 and 2 (1997) and *Managing Corporate Relations* (1998). He is currently establishing director development pro-grammes in Tokyo in association with the Japan Management Association.

EDITORIAL ADVISER

Roger Glanville has a master's degree in further and higher education and is a fellow of the Chartered Institute of Personnel and Development. He was previously the director of academic affairs responsible for all staff training and development at a college of higher education. Since 1989 he has worked as an editor and writer for Open College, Henley Distance Learning, TVU and IoD, and for car companies such as BMW, Citroën, Volkswagen, Nissan, Ford and Jaguar.

OTHER CONTRIBUTORS

Judith Barras is a Principle Lecturer and Programme Manager for the Master's degree in Company Direction at Leeds Business School, Leeds Metropolitan University.

Julian Clover is an officer of the Association of Management Education and Development.

Jerry Rhodes is a consultant and author.

Philip Stiles is a senior research associate at the Judge Institute of Management Studies at the University of Cambridge.

Mahen Tampoe is an independent management consultant and visiting fellow at Henley Management College.

Bernard Taylor is emeritus professor and executive director of the Centre for Board Effectiveness at Henley Management College.

Foreword

This book is a **must** read for managers, aspiring directors and even boardroom veterans who think they have seen it all!

There is now ample evidence that high quality governance goes hand in hand with good performance. This is not about 'box-ticking' governance or the minimal requirements of the Combined Code. Obviously, these minimum levels of governance are essential in order to establish the legitimacy of the role of business enterprises, particularly in these times of scepticism and suspicion about the impact of businesses on communities. However, this book addresses governance in its broadest and most wholesome definition. It is a useful checklist and 'teach-in' about how directors should go about their business in the boardroom and in the organization as a whole. It is about the need to address the constantly changing external environment of the enterprise as well as the internal needs. It is about recognizing and honouring the accountability to shareholders and other stakeholders. It is about the constant task of matching limited resources with opportunities and the application of disciplined strategic thinking and performance management; and it is about the importance of coaching, training, motivating and mentoring that cadre of managers who are future candidates for the Board.

The book addresses the 'collective' decision making that should take place within unitary boards. Britain is one of the few major industrial countries that truly employ unitary boards to manage its enterprises. Indeed, the collective responsibility of the board in this country is deeply enshrined in law and custom.

There are endless debates about the relative merits of our system vis-à-vis the supervisory boards employed on the Continent and there are frequent comparisons with the North American model. In actual practice, US boards – with little representation by executive directors and larger boards on average than our own – bear a closer resemblance to Continental supervisory boards. However, our British model clearly requires skills in collective and collegiate behaviour.

High quality governance is not a luxury solely for large plcs. These important principles are equally applicable to the boards of medium and smaller-sized companies. Indeed, we increasingly see managerial structures and units below board level employing these same principles in their behaviour.

Finally, the 'teach-in' provided by this book addresses these same issues in the public and the not-for-profit sectors.

Richard V Giordano, KBE
Chairman, BG Group plc

Preface

The idea for this book grew out of a series of high-level seminars run by the Association of Management Education and Development (AMED) and the Institute of Directors (IoD) in the 1990s, which involved the major contributors. At these seminars, experienced directors talked about their work in the development of the knowledge, skills and competencies of their fellow directors and their boards. Many of the approaches described by the speakers were successful, but all the approaches were different. From these meetings a working group evolved who kept note of questions the seminars generated. When three years of work had been accumulated, the group decided it would like to record its progress. This book contains a view of the joint experiences of the writers, and focuses on development processes within boards and the role of the developer in supporting directors and boards to work developmentally. The authors recognize that this is an evolving area and that there are no easy solutions.

IS THIS BOOK FOR YOU?

On the following pages you'll find some excellent advice on what a board of directors is supposed to do. You'll see how individual directors and boards can develop themselves and improve their working methods. You'll also be able to read many success stories from industry, business, public sector and charities. The topics we cover include:

- what a board is supposed to do;

- your role as a director;

- the benefits of director and board development;

- organization learning and development;

- board development;

- director development;

- the role of the developer;

- public sector and not-for-profit organizations.

Company directors

You will find this book extremely helpful if you are a company director. The directors we refer to lead companies ranging from the largest of global plcs, through small and medium enterprises (known as SMEs) to very small, private, family-owned businesses. We are aware that most companies are small – 65 per cent of companies have a turnover of less than £250,000 and only 2 per cent have a turnover of more than £5 million. There were over 1.2 million private companies registered at Companies House on 31 March 1999, and we have ensured that the advice we give is relevant to the needs of directors of these types of companies.

Directors of governing bodies within the public and not-for-profit sectors

You will also find this book extremely helpful if you are a director on one of the over 300,000 governing bodies within the public and not-for-profit sectors. These directors govern organizations ranging from very small charities, through schools to large local public spending bodies such as NHS trusts and higher education corporations. In Chapter 8 we deal with particular issues faced by these organizations but, in any case, all the strategy, leadership and development issues are identical to those met in companies.

Relevant director roles

Like many other directors, you may be an experienced, well-qualified manager who has been appointed to the board. With no further advice or training you suddenly realize you're not clear about your new responsibilities. This book is definitely for you, then, if you are:

▌ a director and you wish to improve your effectiveness;

▌ the chairman of a board and you wish to develop the effectiveness of your board;[1]

▌ a potential or aspiring director;

▌ a human resource practitioner with responsibility for senior executive and director development;

▌ a postgraduate student in organization development or human resource development;

▌ a participant on an executive or director development programme.

YOUR WAKE-UP CALL

Take just two minutes to tick 'True' or 'False' against each of the eight statements overleaf. The answers are on page xviii so you can cheat if you're really stuck!

---

[1] The word 'chairman' is used throughout the book since this term is employed in the Companies Act. The term does not denote gender.

	True	False
1. If the word 'director' is on my business card (eg Marketing Director) but I am not a member of the board of my organization, I do not have the same liabilities as board members.	☐	☐
2. There is no difference between a chief executive and a managing director.	☐	☐
3. If my board has a qualified accountant as financial director, the other members of the board have less responsibility for financial matters within the organization.	☐	☐
4. Non-executive directors have fewer responsibilities than executive directors.	☐	☐
5. Directors of state-owned organizations including quangos, agencies, parastatals and schools are exempt from normal directorial responsibilities.	☐	☐
6. There are few laws affecting director or board activities and very little chance of a director being caught for illegal activity.	☐	☐
7. The purpose and tasks of every board are different.	☐	☐
8. In a limited company the prime responsibility of a director is to the company members, ie shareholders.	☐	☐

WERE YOU RIGHT?

	True	False
1. If the word 'director' is on my business card (eg Marketing Director) but I am not a member of the board of my organization, I do not have the same liabilities as board members.	☐	☑
2. There is no difference between a chief executive and a managing director.	☐	☑
3. If my board has a qualified accountant as financial director, the other members of the board have less responsibility for financial matters within the organization.	☐	☑
4. Non-executive directors have fewer responsibilities than executive directors.	☐	☑
5. Directors of state-owned organizations including quangos, agencies, parastatals and schools are exempt from normal directorial responsibilities.	☐	☑
6. There are few laws affecting director or board activities and very little chance of a director being caught for illegal activity.	☐	☑
7. The purpose and tasks of every board are different.	☐	☑
8. In a limited company the prime responsibility of a director is to the company members, ie shareholders.	☐	☑

So, all the statements are false. You'll find a full explanation of each of the reasons in Appendix 1 at the back of the book. But you might as well read the rest of the book anyway. We're sure you'll find it invaluable.

1

What a board is supposed to do

Let's look first at the purpose of a board of directors in a company. Then we can consider their dilemmas and a simple framework to establish their key tasks and analyse their activities.

THE BOARD OF A COMPANY

Consider this quote from the IoD's *Standards for Good Practice for Boards* (1999): 'The key purpose of the board is to ensure the company's prosperity by collectively directing the company's affairs whilst meeting the appropriate interests of its shareholders and relevant stakeholders.' You can see some key words included in this quote. The board of directors makes decisions collectively about issues that determine the company's survival and prosperity. Obviously, the shareholders own the business and the stakeholders include the citizens of the country and their government. As a director, then, you must ensure that the company complies with the various laws, regulations and obligations required of it.

The board also provides leadership to the organization by setting its direction and pace, and by developing its culture and ethics. As a director you are a statutory agent of the company, but you are not a delegate or representative of the shareholders even though they ultimately appointed you. Even if you hold a substantial shareholding you must act as a member of the board of directors and you must play your part in the stewardship of the company. The board needs to be an effective group; it is not a club, nor a committee, nor a mere business formality.

BOARDROOM DILEMMAS

You'll often find conflicting pressures on you. Some tasks of the board are to do with the performance of the company; others are to do with conformance with the law and other standards. Some require the board to be inward-looking; others require the board to be outward-looking. Some are future-focused; others are past- and present-focused. As a result most boards are continuously faced with dilemmas:

- The board must simultaneously be entrepreneurial and drive the business forward while keeping it under prudent control.

- The board has to know enough about the company's workings to answer for its actions, yet be able to stand back from the day-to-day management and retain an objective long-term view.

- The board must be sensitive to the pressures of short-term issues and yet be informed about broader and long-term trends.

- The board must be knowledgeable about local issues and yet be aware of national, international and even global opportunities, competition and other influences.

- The board is expected to be focused on the commercial needs of its business while acting responsibly towards its employees, business partners and society as a whole.

Your final dilemma might be that you find it tempting to get involved with short-term, local issues. But this lets you avoid the intellectual challenge of setting up systems to take on board the broader trends and international competition. Addressing these short-term, local issues can feel more like real work than abstract conceptualization does. However, you'll see below that you have to deal frequently with abstract concepts if you're going to give effective direction.

Dealing with these dilemmas is easier if you have a framework of key tasks to guide you.

THE FOUR KEY TASKS OF THE BOARD

There are four key tasks of the board:

1. establishing the purpose, vision and values;

2. setting strategy and structure;

3. delegating to management;

4. exercising accountability to shareholders and being responsible to relevant stakeholders.

To perform these tasks as a director you will need to carry out an inward examination of the component parts of the company and an outward examination of the commercial and competitive environment. In addition you should be able both to focus on the future of the business and to concentrate on current performance. In Table 1.1 you can see the tasks of the board on a two-by-two matrix.

Table 1.1 *The tasks of the board*

	Past- and Present-orientated	Future-orientated
Outward-looking	4. Exercising accountability to shareholders and responsibility to other interested parties	1. Foresight – determining purpose, vision and values
Inward-looking	3. Oversight – delegating to management	2. Setting strategy and structure

Over the next few pages you'll see each of these four concepts explained and illustrated. You might find it helpful to note some examples of how each of them works currently on your board.

1 Outward-looking, future-orientated

Foresight focuses on determining the organization's purpose, vision and values. These guide the direction and set the pace for its current operations and future development.

The following example shows the purpose, vision and values for Anglian Water plc.

Anglian Water plc

Purpose – the business we are in
To sustain and enhance the lives of our customers through profitable management of water and waste water. We manage water and waste water for our customers through the proactive design and operation of safe, sustainable products and systems. We also sell related products and services to domestic, developer, commercial and industrial markets in the UK and in selected areas of the world.

Vision – what we want to be
The Anglian Water Group will be a winner in the competitive markets of the 21st century by becoming the customers' first choice. We will become the leading water and waste water company in the UK by 2002 and one of the foremost water companies in the world by 2007.

Values – how we should behave to achieve our vision
To contribute to the key business drivers of customer loyalty, quality and efficiency we will work as one team by being:

▊ effective – do the right thing, get it right first time;

▊ competitive – be ready for competition, be open to change, be innovative, be efficient;

▊ responsible – fair to our customers and employees, contribute to the well-being of communities and sustainable development, and operate the business as if we owned it ourselves;

- responsive – give the service we would expect ourselves, learn from ourselves and others, continuously improve the business;

- friendly – in our approach to customers, colleagues and others.

The following quotations will help you see the relevance of looking forward and outwards:

- 'We start with our purpose. Who are we? What sort of business are we in? What are the characteristics of those businesses? What are the limits – in terms of our values and financial boundaries – to the sorts of activities that we are prepared to undertake? What makes our company distinctive?' (Browne, CEO at BP, quoted in Prokesch, 1997: 168).

- 'Organisational design is widely misconstrued as moving boxes and lines. The first task of organisational design concerns designing the governing ideas of purpose, vision and values' (O'Brien, CEO of Hanover Insurance, quoted in Senge, 1998: 588).

- 'You can buy talent, you can buy technology but the key to making the business exciting and distinctive is how you pull it all together and that is a cultural thing' (Orie Dudley, CEO of Scottish Widows Investment Management, quoted in Targett, 2000).

- 'Anyone who tells you that you can change the culture quickly is wrong. It takes at least five years' (Stormont, Group HR Director, Britax Plc, quoted in *Director*, June 2000).

2 Inward-looking, future-orientated

Setting strategy and structure involves:

- reviewing opportunities, threats and risks in the external environment and evaluating their likely effect on the business;

- assessing current and future strengths, weaknesses and risks within the organization;

▌ selecting the strategic options to pursue, and deciding how to implement them;

▌ establishing the business plans;

▌ making sure the organization's structure and resources can support the strategy.

As you'll see from these points and the next quote, the board designs the strategy and support systems, but does not itself implement them. 'Our strategic planning process is designed to keep ideas flowing and stimulate thinking. We see strategy as applying a series of frameworks that help us constantly re-examine what the world can offer and what our competitors are doing' (Browne, CEO at BP, quoted in Prokesch, 1997: 168).

An example of Anglian Water plc strategy is outlined below.

Strategy – how we will achieve our vision and goals

Our strategy to achieve the vision is to:

▌ become the customer's first choice;

▌ grow the business;

▌ deliver superior shareholder returns;

▌ value and recognize employees, enabling them to achieve their full potential.

---

3 Inward-looking, past- and present-orientated

Oversight and delegating to management involve:

▌ delegating authority to management to implement the policies, strategies and business plans;

▌ setting the criteria, and monitoring and evaluating the implementation;

▌ communicating with senior management.

After setting the strategy the board needs to delegate implementation to its managers. 'The top management team must stimulate the organisation, not control it. Its role is to provide strategic directives, to encourage learning and to make sure there are mechanisms for transferring the lessons' (Browne, CEO at BP, quoted in Prokesch, 1997).

4 Outward-looking, past- and present-orientated

Exercising accountability to shareholders and being responsible to relevant stakeholders involve:

▪ ensuring that communications both to and from shareholders and stakeholders are effective;

▪ understanding and taking into account the interests of shareholders and stakeholders;

▪ monitoring relations with shareholders and stakeholders;

▪ promoting the good will and support of the shareholders and stakeholders.

Few boards fulfil all of the tasks in the framework well. 'Any organisation that thinks it does everything the best and need not learn from others is incredibly arrogant and foolish' (Browne, CEO at BP, quoted in Prokesch, 1997: 147).

Some company boards have produced formal statements of these responsibilities. Here is an example, from Luke March (1999), formerly Director of Corporate Governance at BT.

The role of the board at BT

The board of directors at BT have formally identified the following roles of the board:

1. setting direction:

   — vision, mission, values and ethics;

2. approve:

    —   strategic plans;

    —   annual operating and capital expenditure plan;

    —   projects over £100 million;

    —   acquisitions and disposals over £100 million;

    —   dividends;

3. oversight and control:

    —   operating and financial performance;

    —   changes to accounting practices;

    —   internal controls;

    —   compliance (securities, legal regulatory);

4. public policy issues:

    —   stakeholder issues;

    —   shareholder communications;

    —   employee share schemes;

    —   pensions provision.

How does this compare with any statement your board has approved and issued? You may be nodding wisely at this point and thinking your board seems to have all the issues well in hand. That may make you feel good, but unfortunately the list isn't yet complete. We've only dealt with responsibilities. Now you need to consider the board's powers.

RESERVED POWERS

Some companies have created a statement of reserved powers. This is to make clear which particular powers in the company the board reserves for its own decision-making processes. It never delegates these to any level of management. These statements are becoming regarded as evidence of good practice in corporate governance. A survey of financial investment institutions by Pensions Investment Research Consultants Ltd (PIRC) in January 2000 revealed that 29 out of the 38 institutions surveyed had a statement of reserved powers. Here is an example from a large public limited company.

A sample statement of matters to be reserved for the approval of the board

Companies Act

▪ Approval of interim and final statements.

▪ Approval of the interim dividend and recommendation of the final dividend.

▪ Approval of any significant changes in accounting policies.

▪ Appointment or removal of the company secretary.

▪ Recommendations for the appointment and removal of auditors and setting of their remuneration.

Stock Exchange

▪ Approval of all circulars and listing publications.

▪ Approval of press releases concerning matters decided by the board.

Management

▪ Formulation of corporate strategy.

▪ Approval of business plans and forecasts.

▪ Changes relating to capital structure or company status.

▪ Appointments to subsidiary company boards.

▪ Changes to the management structure of the group.

▪ Arrangements for the system of internal control.

▌ Prosecution, defence or settlement of litigation.

▌ Major capital expenditure and asset disposals with a value in excess of £x, the amount to be determined by the board annually.

▌ Acquisitions and disposals of companies or businesses.

▌ Treasury policies.

▌ Risk management strategy.

▌ Contracts not in the ordinary course of business.

Board and board committees

▌ Appointment and removal of directors.

▌ Approval of the terms and conditions of appointment of directors and their terms of reference.

▌ Formation, terms of reference and membership of board committee.

Miscellaneous

▌ Major changes affecting the company pension scheme (major rule changes, change in fund manager, pension increases, changes in membership of the trust company).

▌ Changes to share option schemes and the grant of share options.

▌ Approval and changes to health and safety policy.

▌ Approval and changes to environmental policy.

▌ Approval and changes to employment policy.

As you can see, the list is substantial. You might think it a good idea at this stage to make a list of all the responsibilities and reserved powers that are relevant to your board. You can then discuss them with the company secretary and chairman (especially if you occupy one of these posts!) to determine how they are, or should be, handled.

SUMMARY

The key purpose of the board is to ensure the company's prosperity by collectively directing the company's affairs whilst meeting the appropriate interests of its shareholders and relevant stakeholders. This involves:

▌ establishing the purpose, vision and values of the organization;

▌ setting strategy and structure;

▌ delegating to management;

▌ exercising accountability to relevant stakeholders.

Statements of reserved powers have been developed by some boards to clarify the particular powers in the company that the board reserves for its own decision-making processes.

2

Your role as a director

The directors determine whether or not a company survives and thrives. The extent to which the board liberates or constrains the energies and talents of the people of a company is determined by the competence of the directors and how effectively they work together (Peter Morgan, former Director General of the Institute of Directors).

The law makes no distinction between directors. The four main positions on a company board of directors are:

▌ chairman;

▌ managing director;

▌ executive director;

▌ non-executive director.

These are therefore convenient, rather than legal, titles. The Companies Act 1985 does, however, require every private and public company to have a company secretary, but company secretaries do not have to be board members. We'll look at each of these positions in turn.

WHAT A CHAIRMAN DOES

As we have seen, the main task of the board is to set the direction and strategy for the company. The basic responsibility of the chairman is to ensure that the board is effective in this task. This means that the board should concentrate on directing the company and not on managing it.

The chairman has a key role in leadership. This involves getting all the directors involved in discussions and decisions, and monitoring the contribution of individual directors. The chairman has to ensure the board's agenda is appropriate and focuses on the key tasks. In particular, the chairman has to ensure that the board monitors the company's progress but does not slide into managing the business – we are repeating this point because it is so important.

The chairman must monitor the composition and structure of the board itself by regularly reviewing:

- the overall size of the board;

- the balance between non-executive and executive directors;

- the balance of age, experience and personality of the directors.

If the composition and structure are inappropriate, the chairman is responsible for initiating development processes. The chairman also has an important development role with regard to all directors.

The chairman has the task of preparing for and chairing the meetings of the board, and co-ordinating the timing and frequency of meetings. This includes ensuring that board members have relevant and up-to-date information on the progress of the company.

Shareholders can agree to dispense with annual general meetings (AGMs) and the approval of the annual accounts in private companies. For public companies and private companies that retain AGMs, the chairman is required under the Companies Act to make statements at the AGM to shareholders and to indicate how the company is progressing. The chairman also has a wider representational role and has to put across the company's aims and policies to all those whose confidence in the business is important.

Finally, the chairman must initiate regular reviews of board performance, and establish a programme of development processes for the board and individual members.

Hugh Parker, a former Managing Director of the McKinsey London office, summarized the role of chairman as follows:

▌ *Chairmanship is a highly subjective activity not an exact science subject to any fixed rules or laws.*

    Every successful chairman does it his way and these ways can and do differ widely. It is therefore not possible to prescribe anything but the broadest generalizations just how the chairman's role should be performed.

▌ *Every successful chairman is by definition a leader.*

    Without this quality of personal leadership, however that is defined, the vital process of corporate renewal – making tomorrow's company out of today's – is unlikely to occur. Indeed it almost certainly will not, and the company will sooner or later fail or be taken over.

▌ *The role of chairman has become increasingly complex and internationally competitive.*

▌ *The only way that any chairman can hope to cope with these future conditions is through teamwork.*

Sir John Harvey Jones's observation that 'the job of corporate governance is too great for any chairman to do alone. That is why you need a board. The chairman's primary job is to create and work with a strong board' is I believe the key to the dilemma. A wise chairman will not attempt to be a one man band, for all the obvious reasons: it is too risky for the company: it is unfair to himself and his colleagues: and in today's world it is simply impossible. He must create and use his board wisely because it is the board as a whole that must ultimately bear the full weight of corporate governance and renewal. That is the true meaning of the title 'Chairman of the Board'.

(IoD, 1991: A4, 15–16)

What are the features of a well-run board?

A board that exhibits 'good practice' will probably:

▌ have a good balance of well-chosen and competent directors;

▌ meet regularly under the leadership of the chairman;

▌ have challenging agendas and minutes that are correctly kept;

▌ shape the destiny of the company;

▌ focus on the four key tasks of the board – determining purpose, vision and values; setting strategy and structure; delegating to management; and exercising accountability to members and responsibility to interested parties;

▌ have board induction, inclusion, competence building and appraisal systems in place.

What are the features of a poorly run board?

A board that exhibits 'poor practice' will probably:

▌ be wrongly structured in that it is too big or too small;

▌ have insufficient range of expertise;

▌ contain directors with executive responsibilities who see their role as protecting their own turf;

▌ be provided with inadequate information (often this information will only focus upon the financial activities of the organization and fail to provide any information on customers, the marketplace, operational efficiency, learning and development within the organization);

▌ take major decisions with inadequate debate or no challenge (it is a 'country club' board that will not take hard and unpleasant, but necessary, decisions – the board meetings are social occasions over a good lunch, with inadequate time for discussion, and a rubber-stamping of decisions);

▌ have decisions overturned by a dominant individual;

▌ have decisions made by cabals of the board;

▌ have decisions made outside the board;

▌ have few, if any, reviews to see if the decisions were correct or not;

▌ fail to push management hard on succession, investment (including training), R & D, or product or market development;

▌ fail to keep the company's financing arrangements under review: the wrong banks, too many banks, the wrong means of finance, the wrong structure of indebtedness, the wrong risk profile.

WHAT A MANAGING DIRECTOR DOES

The titles 'chief executive' and 'managing director' are purely descriptive ones and in themselves carry no legal significance or obligations. The chief executive is the senior full-time executive in the business. In some cases the chief executive reports to the board but may not be a member of the board. In this case the individual would not be able to use the title 'managing director' since this title explicitly suggests to people within and outside the company that the person is a director and therefore a member of the board. In this book we use the term 'managing director' rather than 'chief executive'.

The key role of the managing director is to take the lead in putting the long-term strategy into operation. This involves having to:

▌ develop strategic operating plans that reflect the longer-term objectives and priorities established by the board;

▌ maintain an ongoing dialogue with the chairman of the board;

▌ put in place adequate operational planning and financial control systems;

▌ ensure that the operating objectives and standards of performance are not only understood but also owned by the management and other employees;

▌ closely monitor the operating and financial results against plans and budgets;

▌ take remedial action where necessary and inform the board of significant changes;

▌ maintain the operational performance for the company.

'The key managerial task of the CEO is not to know everything but to build an executive team that can get the whole job done' (Senge, 1998: 585).

If the managing director commits the company outside the limits of delegated authority, the company can sue the managing director. This is the ultimate constraint on his or her authority.

WHAT DIRECTORS DO

The activity of managing a business has been defined as: 'the process of planning, organising, leading and controlling the efforts of organisation members and of using all other organisational resources to achieve stated organisational goals' (Mescon, Albert and Khedouri, 1985). However, many researchers (such as Mintzberg, 1975) have analysed the activities that they have observed directors carrying out. They found that they did not fit easily into a classification system based upon planning, organizing, leading and controlling activities.

Instead, researchers focused upon the role that the individuals played within specific contexts. Research into the behaviour of directors within a board has shown that both executive and non-executive directors can play different roles. The roles and their related activities may be as shown in Table 2.1.

You will know from your own experience that many of these roles rely on informal processes. So the straight application of rules or comparisons with what happens in other organizations will not help any analysis. Nor will rules automatically improve your board's effectiveness. However, you may be able to review the composition of your board to ensure that all these role activities are undertaken. You may then wish to review the attributes of the individual members.

Table 2.1 *The roles of a director*

Role	Activity
Decision maker	Evaluate strategic options and decide upon particular courses of action.
	Make an objective assessment of a situation.
	See board matters from an external and independent point of view (non-executives).

Table 2.1 *The roles of a director (continued)*

Role	Activity
Representative	Protect the interests of other parties such as shareholders (non-executives).
	Look out for the interests of the party that put them on the board (nominee directors).
Challenger	Question the board's assumptions.
	Surface conflicts, vested interests or personal agendas that might lead to turf wars.
	Cause change in others' thinking by challenging their beliefs about the company, its markets and its competitors.
	Use rigorous analysis to stimulate the board discussions with new, alternative insights and ideas.
Supervisor of executive management	Supervise, monitor and evaluate executive management's implementation of policies, strategies and business plans (non-executives).
	Determine monitoring criteria.
	Ensure that the internal control procedures provide reliable, valid and timely information.
Reflective listener	Act as reflective listener for other directors, the chief executive or chairman (non-executives). Share concerns about issues (often interpersonal problems) outside the boardroom.
Process manager	Act as safety valve at times of crisis or conflict, in order to release the pressure, prevent further damage and save the situation.
	Ensure that both formal and informal board processes are appropriate and being used.

Table 2.1 *The roles of a director (continued)*

Role	Activity
Knowledge provider	Bring specialist or professional skills, knowledge and experience to bear on issues such as market opportunities, new technologies, industry developments.
	Use personal contacts to connect the board and top management into networks of potentially useful people and organizations.
Company representative	Represent the company externally with fund managers, financial analysts, industry gatherings, the media, etc.
Status provider	Add status rather than make any contribution to board deliberations.
Maverick	Think outside the box – creative, imaginative and unorthodox individuals who are big picture visionaries and ignore detail.
Developer	Participate in the development of the effectiveness of individual directors and the overall working of the board.

The attributes of a director

The Institute of Directors (1999) have identified the following personal attributes as being important to be represented at the board:

Strategic perception

- change orientation;
- creativity;
- foresight;

- organizational awareness;
- perspective;
- strategic awareness;

Decision making

- critical faculty;
- decisiveness;
- judgement;

Analysis and the use of information

- consciousness of detail;
- eclecticism;
- numeracy;
- problem recognition;

Communication

- listening skills;
- openness;
- verbal fluency;
- presentation skills;
- written communication skills;
- responsiveness;

Interaction with others

- confidence;
- co-ordination skills;
- flexibility;
- presence;
- integrity;
- learning ability;
- motivation;
- persuasiveness;
- sensitivity;

Achievement of results

- business acumen;
- delegation skills;
- exemplar;
- drive;
- resilience;
- risk acceptance;
- tenacity.

You can now see that the individuals on the board have to work well with one another as a team, as well as making their individual contributions. The two lists – activities and attributes – give you the chance to map your own board to check that all the competencies you need are actually represented.

Recent research

Dulewicz and Herbert (1999) from Henley Management College tracked the career progress of general managers to directorial positions over a seven-year period. Almost all of the high-flyer group became directors over the period and were receiving an average salary of £80,000. Data was collected on 100 participants using two questionnaires: 1) occupational personality questionnaire (OPQ concept 5); and 2) job competencies survey. You can see the characteristics that differentiated the high-flyers in Table 2.2 overleaf.

The researchers concluded that:

> *The high fliers appear to be rather hard nosed, calculating individuals but most managers would not be too surprised to learn that those who advance most rapidly to the top are: effective planners and organizers who take actions involving clear risk; show vision, inspiration, commitment and enthusiasm; who develop, appraise, direct and take charge of their staff; who are ascendant, forceful and decisive and who set demanding goals for self and others, see things through to completion, play to win and who are determined to beat others. Many academics and consultants, however, will be disappointed to learn that performance on some of the softer competencies and personality factors concerned with, for example, interpersonal relationships and integrity does not appear to lead to rapid advancement to the top.*

(*Dulewicz and Herbert, 1999: 20*)

Transformational leadership

This interesting term has been devised by researchers (Tichy and Ulrich, 1984) to describe the qualities and behaviour of directors who are driven to create change within a board. Transformational leadership is characterized by the directors:

▪ seeing themselves as change agents and setting out to make a difference by transforming the organization;

▪ having the courage to deal with resistance, take a stand, take risks and confront reality;

▪ believing in people's motivation, trust and empowerment;

▪ being driven by a strong sense of values;

▪ viewing their own and others' mistakes as learning opportunities;

Table 2.2 *The profile of a high-flyer*

Characteristics	
Intellectual Planning and organizing	Plans priorities, assignments and the allocation of resources.
	Organizes resources efficiently and effectively.
	Delegates work to the appropriate staff.
Risk taking	Takes or initiates action that involves a deliberate gamble in order to achieve a recognized benefit or advantage.
	Seeks new experiences and situations rather than the security afforded by well-established or familiar ones.
Interpersonal Managing staff	Adopts appropriate styles for achieving group objectives.
	Monitors and evaluates staff's work.
	Shows vision and inspiration.
	Develops the skills and competencies of staff.
Controlling	Takes charge, directs, manages, organizes and supervises others.
Motivating others	Inspires others to achieve goals by showing vision and a clear idea of what needs to be achieved. Shows commitment and enthusiasm.
Assertiveness and decisiveness	Is ascendant, and forceful in dealing with others.
	Can take charge.
	Is willing to take risks, decisive, ready to take decisions even on limited information.
Results orientation Achievement – motivation	Sets demanding goals for self and others and is dissatisfied with average performance.
	Makes full use of own time and resources.
	Sees a task through to completion irrespective of obstacles and set-backs.
Competitive	Plays to win, is determined to beat others, is a poor loser.

■ having the ability to cope with complexity, uncertainty and ambiguity;

■ helping members to conceptualize, craft, articulate and ensure the implementation of the board's vision.

Having too many of these people on the board might not be too much fun if you're the chairman, but you need one or two to complement the range of other types and any possible complacency. You need also to be aware of the interactions on the board as a basis for development.

Research in top teams

In 2000, Andrew Kakabadse from Cranfield published the results of one of the largest surveys ever undertaken. It was conducted over seven years and covered almost 10,000 companies and public sector organizations in 15 countries. It revealed that poor strategic decisions often not spotted for several years have cost shareholders hundreds of millions of pounds in lost profits. His research involving attitudes of CEOs, chairmen and MDs highlighted that: 1) 30 per cent of respondents in the UK felt that members of the senior executive held fundamentally different views as to the direction of the company; and 2) 47 per cent of respondents in the UK felt that there were issues or sensitivities that merited, but did not receive, attention within the top team. Further analysis of the findings indicated that:

■ top executive work is conducted in groupings;

■ too much individualism can be destructive for the business;

■ success was derived from there being a broad experience of functions in the business.

Sustaining momentum in top team development was built around the following interventions:

■ feedback;

■ team feedback;

■ third-party facilitation;

■ the promotion of high achievers;

■ training;

■ presentation skills to communicate consistently a coherent set of beliefs and values;

■ time for personal development.

The danger of groupthink

The work of Janis (1982) warns boards about groupthink. This term refers to the defective decision making that occurs in cohesive groups. It is normally caused by the group overestimating their power, having closed minds or a pressure towards unanimity. The symptoms of groupthink are:

▪ *an overestimation of the group's power and morality* – this frequently provides an illusion of invulnerability shared by most or all of the members, which can create excessive optimism and can also encourage the group to take extreme risks, eg acquisitions;

▪ *an unquestioned belief in the group's inherent morality* – there is an inclination of the group to ignore ethical and moral consequences of their decisions;

▪ *the discounting of warnings* – groupthink can often lead to the discounting of warnings and other information that might lead to the members reconsidering their assumptions;

▪ *stereotyping the 'enemy'* – stereotyped views of the 'enemy' (eg competitors) and a belief that the leaders of these organizations are stupid;

▪ *self-censorship* – self-censorship of deviations from the apparent group consensus reflecting each member's inclination to minimize his or her doubts;

▪ *a shared illusion of unanimity* – a shared illusion of unanimity concerning judgements conforming to the majority view (partly resulting from self-censorship of deviations augmented by the false assumption that silence means consent);

▪ *lack of dissent* – direct pressure on any member who expresses arguments against any of the group illusions, stereotypes or commitments making clear that this type of dissent is contrary to what is expected of all loyal members;

▪ *'mind guards'* – the emergence of self-appointed mind guards who protect the group from adverse information that might shatter their shared complacency.

You can reduce groupthink with positive action. Your chairman might assign the role of critical evaluator to each member and encourage the group to give high priority to airing objections and doubts. Of course, the chairman would have to be prepared to accept criticism particularly over the processes employed to manage disagreements. Alfred Sloan, a former chairman of General Motors, is reported as saying: 'Gentlemen, I take it we are all in agreement on the decision here… Then I postpone further discussion of this matter until our next meeting to give ourselves time to develop disagreement and perhaps gain some understanding of what the decision is all about' (Janis, 1982: 271). At every meeting devoted to evaluating policy alternatives, at least one member of the group should be assigned the role of devil's advocate.

Directors and managers – there is a difference

One of the key issues to emerge from management research over the last 20 years is that there are many fundamental differences between being a director and being a manager. It's not a trivial matter like a new job title and a shorter walk from your parking bay to the directors' lift and dining room. The differences are substantial and quite onerous.

In a recent survey (IoD, 1998b) directors were asked to distinguish between 'direction' and 'management'. Key factors for direction included:

▪ strategic awareness or thinking;

▪ vision;

▪ leadership;

▪ long-term dimension;

▪ 'big picture' or objective;

▪ communications dimension.

You can see a more detailed summary of the major differences between direction and management in Table 2.3

Table 2.3 *The major differences between directors and managers*

	Directors	Managers
Decision Making	Directors are required to determine the future of the organization and protect its assets and reputation. They also need to consider how their decisions relate to stakeholders and the regulatory framework.	Management is concerned with implementing the decisions and the policies made by the board.
Duties and Responsibilities	Directors, not managers, have the ultimate responsibility for the long-term prosperity of the company. Directors are required in law to apply skill and care in exercising their duty to the company and are subject to fiduciary duties. If they are in breach of their duties or act improperly, directors may be made personally liable in both civil and criminal law. On occasion, directors can be held responsible for acts of the company.	Managers are not bound by these legal responsibilities.
Relationship with Shareholders	The directors of a company can be removed from office by the shareholders. In addition, the directors of a company are accountable for the company to the shareholders.	Managers are usually appointed and dismissed by directors or management and usually have no legal requirement to be held to account.

	Directors	*Managers*
Leadership	It is the board of directors who must provide the intrinsic leadership and direction at the top of the organization.	While the day-to-day leadership of the company is in the hands of the managing director or chief executive, managers are acting on behalf of the directors.
Ethics and Values	The board has a key role in the determination of the values and ethical position of the company.	The management must enact the ethos, taking its direction from the board.
Company Administration	Directors are responsible for the company's administration.	The related duties associated with company administration can be delegated to management but this does not relieve the directors of the ultimate responsibility for it.
Statutory Provisions	If a company becomes insolvent, the Insolvency Act 1986 imposes various duties and responsibilities on directors that may involve personal liability, criminal prosecution and disqualification. There are numerous other statutory provisions that can create offences of strict liability under which directors may face penalties if the company fails to comply.	These statutory provisions do not affect managers.

SUMMARY

The effectiveness of the board depends on the competence of the directors and on how effectively they work together. The features of a well-run board include:

▊ having a good balance of well-chosen and competent directors;

▊ meeting regularly under the leadership of the chairman;

▊ having challenging agendas and minutes that are correctly kept;

▊ shaping the destiny of the company;

▊ focusing on the four key tasks of the board – determining purpose, vision and values, setting strategy and structure, delegating to management and exercising accountability to members and responsibility to interested parties;

▊ having board induction, inclusion, competence building and appraisal systems in place.

When considering the balance of the board you should remember that all directors adopt roles. As a result of the issues raised in this chapter you might wish to consider your own board and ask yourself the following questions:

▊ Does every director provide at least one role?

▊ Are any roles so under- or over-represented that we should consider changing the composition of the board?

▊ Is any one director playing an over-dominant role on the board?

▊ Is the board expecting too much of that person?

3

The benefits of director and board development

There are many forces driving director and board development. The key drivers include: 1) the superior organization performance and sharper competitive edge that are expected to be the result; and 2) the desire of directors to be more professional in the performance of their board activities.

The first of these is a presumption that is only fulfilled if you have excellently designed and executed development processes. The second may be attributed to the law requiring directors to behave in a professional manner. In particular, directors are being held to account for their decisions and actions by shareholders and other stakeholders. The second may also be attributed to the desire of directors to avoid a scandal and remain out of the public eye. The drivers and outputs of director and board development are shown in Figure 3.1.

USING BOARD DEVELOPMENT AS A SOURCE OF COMPETITIVE EDGE

Successful companies create jobs, create wealth and divide the value added among those contributing to their success. The drive and

Drivers   **Outputs**

```
┌─────────────────────────────────┐                    ┌──────────────────┐
│ Using board development as a key │                    │    Individual    │
│ source of superior organization │                    │   improvement    │
│ performance leading to competitive│                   └──────────────────┘
│ edge.                            │
└─────────────────────────────────┘     ┌──────────────────┐  ┌──────────────────┐
                                         │ Director and board│  │      Board       │
                                         │   development    │  │   improvement    │
┌─────────────────────────────────┐     └──────────────────┘  └──────────────────┘
│ The desire of directors to be more│
│ professional                     │                    ┌──────────────────┐
│  • Legal compliance              │                    │  Organizational  │
│  • Stakeholder expectations and  │                    │   improvement    │
│    responsibilities              │                    └──────────────────┘
│  • Avoidance of scandals         │
└─────────────────────────────────┘
```

Figure 3.1 *The drivers and outputs of director and board development*

efficiency of these organizations sustain the country's economy. Thus the effectiveness with which their boards discharge their responsibilities contributes significantly to the strength of the UK's competitive position. In the current business environment, boards are free to drive their organizations forward in their chosen manner but they exercise that freedom within a framework of effective accountability.

Today's business environment is undergoing far-reaching and profound change brought about by examples such as:

▌ *Improvements in technology.* E-commerce in the business-to-customer sector is presenting boards with a challenge; do they abandon their current manufacturing and marketing strategy to transform themselves into virtual organizations, continue with their existing operations and establish a totally separate electronic arm, or weld the two strategies together to become a 'clicks and mortar' business?

▌ *Changing markets.* Many organizations have focused on globalization only to find their strategy thwarted by local culture; why did Disney have such great difficulty in transporting their theme park concept from Florida to wet, cold France, and how do car makers standardize production for the markets across Europe when, for example, local desire for external accessories, in-car entertainment, electric windows and automatic transmission varies so widely from country to country?

▌ *Changing work processes.* Development times for new products and services are falling; how do firms maintain the strength of their brands but keep them flexible enough to support frequent model changes (eg Zanussi, Hotpoint)?

▌ *Changes in size.* Large companies go on the acquisition trail; how does the board decide between buying a major competitor to gain the synergy (eg AOL) and splitting its operations to gain fleetness of foot (eg Unilever, ICI)?

▌ *Changes in financing.* Companies respond to a mature industry or slow market growth; how do they decide whether to distribute earnings to shareholders, buy back shares or use funds to invest in newly developing sectors? (See Chapter 9, Case 2: Anglian Water plc.)

▌ *Changes in organization structure.* Virtual organizations are built around knowledge management; how does a board choose a structure that enables the people who operate within it to maintain the human touch that is thought to be the lifeblood of every successful company (eg the Co-operative Bank and smile.com)?

▌ *Increased regulation.* National laws are complemented – and complicated! – by directives from regional, international and world-wide regulatory authorities; how does a company's board keep up to date with details that might turn into very expensive mistakes (eg Microsoft vs US regulatory authorities in 2000 concerning the alleged misuse of monopoly power)?

In this competitive and turbulent environment, boards in companies of every size are required to develop strategies and exploit business opportunities. Director and board development is increasingly being seen as a key element if they are to succeed.

Research case study – training and development linked to board improvement

The Institute of Management (1995) investigated whether leadership training programmes had an impact upon improving board performance. Their survey results were:

No change	6%
Slight change	24%
Moderate improvement	52%
Great improvement	18%

THE DESIRE OF DIRECTORS TO BE MORE PROFESSIONAL

You want to stay out of jail, right? That's the bottom line. So, as a director you normally intend all your actions to be legal at the very least. Above that level most directors express a strong desire to work within the law and avoid the possibility of being sued by aggrieved third parties or being fined by the courts. It is essential you keep up to date with legal changes but the laws concerning director and board activity are numerous and complex. For an outline of legislation, see Table 3.1.

Table 3.1 *Statutory liability of the company director*

Company Legislation	Criminal Justice Act 1993
	Companies Acts 1985 and 1989
	Insolvency Act 1986
	Company Directors Disqualification Act 1986
	European works council regulations
Stock Exchange Requirements for Listed Companies	Combined Code
	Listing Rules
	Mergers and take-overs
Safety	Control of substances hazardous to health regulations (COSHH) 1994
	Health and Safety at Work (HSAW) Act 1974
Employment	Unfair dismissal and statements of reasons for dismissal (variation of qualifying period) order 1999
	EC Directive on working time employment rights 1996 and working time regulations 1998
	Human Rights Act 1998
	Employment Relations Act 1998
	National Minimum Wage Act 1998
	Employment Right (Dispute Resolution) Act 1998

	Employment Rights Act 1996
	Disability Discrimination Act 1995
	Pensions Act 1995
	Sunday Trading Act 1994
	Trade Union and Labour Relations (consolidation) Act (TULRA) 1992
	Wages Act 1986
	Sex Discrimination Acts 1975 and 1986
	Race Relations Act 1976
	Equal Pay Act 1970
	Parental Leave Regulations
	Transfer of undertakings (protection of employment) regulations (TUPE)
	Young people's time off for study and training regulations
	Unfair dismissal compensation limit regulations
	Trade union recognition regulations
	Part time workers regulations
Environmental Law	Environmental Act 1995
	Water Act 1989
	Town and Country Planning Act 1974
	Control of Pollution Act 1974
	Fire Precautions Act 1971
Intellectual Property	Data Protection Act 1998
	Public Interest Disclosure Act 1998
	Patents Act 1977
Consumer Protection	Consumer Protection Act 1987
	Supply of Goods and Services Act 1982
	Sales of Goods Act 1979
	Consumer Credit Act 1974
	Trades Description Act 1968
Competition	Competition Act 1998
Financial	Financial Services Act 2000
	Late Payment of Commercial Debt Interest Act 1998
	Insolvency Act 1986
	Theft Act 1968

The principal circumstances in which you might, as a director, be personally liable include:

▊ *Fraudulent trading.* This occurs where directors conduct the business of the company with dishonest intent to defraud creditors. Directors can be fined and/or imprisoned and can be disqualified from acting as a director for a maximum of 15 years.

▊ *Fraudulent evasion of VAT.* This can occur if a director makes a dishonest declaration or fails to register for VAT.

▊ *Failure to show the company name clearly on company documents.* These documents include: bills of exchange, promissory notes, endorsements, cheques or orders for money.

▊ *Wrongful trading.* This occurs where a director knows, or ought to know, that the company cannot avoid insolvent liquidation and does not take every step to minimize the potential loss to creditors.

▊ *Employment of illegal immigrants and 'over-stayers'.* Under the Asylum and Immigration Act 1996, directors can be fined up to £5,000 for every offence involving the employment of a person who is not entitled to work in the UK.

▊ *Acting as a director whilst disqualified.* When a person acts in contravention of a disqualification order, he or she commits a criminal offence and faces up to two years' imprisonment or an unlimited fine.

▊ *Financial misconduct.* This includes: making false or misleading statements or omitting information from listing particulars or a prospectus; irregularities in share allotment; failure to observe shareholders' rights of pre-emption, and failure to obtain a trading certificate for a public company before entering into a transaction with a third party.

Ignorance of the law cannot be used as a defence in a court of law. So, you may need to consider what steps you can take to increase your knowledge of the law and its potential impact upon you.

Of course, you might think you can give yourself some protection by taking out insurance. But the press and Web sites on the Internet are shining stronger spotlights on incidents of directorial non-competence. In addition, society is becoming more litigious. The result is that directors' and officers' liability insurance rates are rising as successful claims are made. Many directors are seeking ways of reversing these trends. The idea of accreditation and registration of directors seems an attractive way of limiting insurance losses whilst keeping premiums low.

Let's now consider steps you might take in your efforts to ensure the wishes of all interested parties are met.

KEEPING THE IMPORTANT STAKEHOLDERS HAPPY

Stakeholders' expectations concerning an organization's performance are becoming ever more demanding. Stakeholders may have expectations concerning the organization's:

▌ financial performance;

▌ environmental performance;

▌ social performance;

Some CEOs and business leaders are beginning to talk of the 'triple bottom line'. Companies like NatWest and General Motors refer to the economic, social and environmental dimensions of sustainability in their corporate environmental reports.

Providers of capital

First of all, you and your colleagues on the board have to enjoy a good relationship with your shareholders and providers of capital:

> *It is important that companies should communicate their strategies to...*
> *shareholders and that their shareholders should understand them. It is*
> *equally important that shareholders should play their part in the*
> *communication process by informing companies if there are aspects of*
> *the business which give them cause for concern. Both shareholders and*
> *directors have to contribute to the building of a sound working relation*
> *ship between them.*

(Cadbury, 1992)

In 1957, private investors owned over 66 per cent of UK shares. By 1998 the picture had changed. Private shareholders by number still dominated share registers of plcs but typically accounted for only 20 per cent of quoted companies' shares. The steep decline in private share-holding has been matched by a reduction in the influence exerted by small shareholders on the companies in which they invest, as well as on the City generally:

> *[Institutions] have much better access to information about what is going on. Private investors are not privy to behind the scenes gossip, such as tip offs from brokers which is passed on routinely to big shareholders. And few can afford to buy the reams of analysis published on major companies. Indeed they may be lucky in future to get even the full annual report and accounts given the growing tendency to send private investors short reports which contain skeleton financial details only. Private investors also lose out when it comes to dealing. Economies of scale mean that smaller trades are expensive to brokers to process – something that is reflected in their charges. The average commission of 0.82% paid by private investors last year is more than 5 times the average 0.16% charged to institutions according to Stock Exchange figures.*

(*Eaglesham, 1998*)

However, an increased level of shareholder activism has been a feature of the last decade. Active shareholders are learning how to form pressure groups, especially through the Internet, to gather proxy votes and play an active role in general meetings by asking questions rather than demonstrating outside the door.

British Gas, 1994

In 1994 Cedric Brown, CEO, was alleged to be 'the most hated man in Britain'. He even had a pig named after him, which was paraded in front of shareholders at the company's annual general meeting. In 1995 John Major, the prime minister, recommended that British Gas shareholders who were unhappy about the chief executive's salary rise should go along to the AGM and complain. The campaign against Mr Brown was caused by a very large increase in salary from £270,000 to £475,000. The annual general meeting at London's Docklands was attended by 4,600 shareholders, 4 MPs and Cedric the pig. The protest resolutions failed because most of the institutional shareholders backed the company.

Interflora, 1997

Interflora co-ordinates flower deliveries across the UK and provides computer terminals and clearing payment services between its members. It has 2,600 members who collectively own the Association of Independent Florists. In 1997 the board proposed to harmonize the flower delivery service throughout the UK and raise florists' annual subscription charges from £300 to £1,750. The members of the Association strongly objected to the moves, arguing that changes would lead to a franchise-based group and undermine their independence. In addition, many of the smaller florists argued that the higher subscriptions would push them out of business. At an extraordinary general meeting in the summer of 1997, 11 directors were deselected.

Shareholder activists now use much better company research, frequently provided by analysts and by pensions and investment research consultants. They also use public relations skills to get media support.

HSBC, 1995

At the 1995 AGM at the Barbican Centre in London the chairman of HSBC had to expel six shareholders for disrupting the meeting, and deal with the adverse publicity of two shareholders protesting at the company's involvement in the arms trade by arriving at the meeting in a military tank.

Vodaphone, 2000

In the summer of 2000, the National Association of Pension Funds publicly stated their concern at the group chief executive's remuneration package of £10 million. At the AGM, almost 30 per cent of Vodaphone shareholders voted against the company's remuneration policy.

Shareholders can exert great power over company boards. But, as you have now seen, it does not happen without some trigger point causing shareholders to organize themselves. The organizations may be of individuals with serious (to them) grievances or of institutions such as Pensions & Investment Research Consultants Limited (PIRC).

In addition, you have more risk assessment by investors and the 'democratization' of pensioner power. Many more relatively poor people now have access to wealth via their pension funds, equity in housing, shares and life insurances. They have an interest in protecting their wealth to hand on to the next generation, who will be even more financially literate. Pension fund owners are now much more demanding of the performance of the companies in which they invest.

Institutional shareholders

If your company is listed on a stock exchange, one of the most important relationships you have to manage is with the institutional shareholders. They include:

▪ life insurance funds;

▪ pension funds;

▪ non-life insurance funds;

▪ investment trusts;

▪ unit trusts.

The media often characterize institutional shareholders as being fixated on companies' short-term results. However, it is not in the fund managers' interest to think only about the short term. Few fund managers are interested in trading on the margin and all seek their ideal of good dividends and capital growth. Institutions usually find it very difficult to sell very large blocks of shares without significantly depressing share price.

NAPF, 1997

In 1997 the National Association of Pension Funds published a survey showing that the average length of time a UK fund manager holds a share is eight years.

When fund managers are disappointed by underperforming boards, they increasingly want to be informed and consulted about board issues such as:

▌ the processes of strategic decision making;

▌ positioning in changing markets;

▌ risk assessment strategies to ensure prudent control mechanisms.

They demand board transparency, better business ethics and fuller accountability. In the UK in the spring of 1997, the fund managers Hermes, RailPen, CalPERS and the National Association of Pension Funds all published independent codes of conduct for corporate governance for listed companies. These complement the official reports:

▌ Cadbury Report on Financial Aspects of Corporate Governance (1992);

▌ Greenbury Report on Directors' Remuneration (1995);

▌ Hampel Report on Corporate Governance (1998);

▌ Turnbull Report on Internal Control (1999).

Many of the above reports' recommendations have been incorporated into the London Stock Exchange Combined Code (1999) that applies to all listed companies in the UK. Perhaps the most important warning if you're on a plc board is that these new independent codes highlight the desire of fund managers to take a more active interest in the competence of the board collectively and individually. In addition, fund managers are increasingly willing to vote on these publicly at general meetings and to publicize their intentions to encourage others to back them by giving them their proxy votes.

CalPERS, 1997

The shaming of directors and boards by institutions is becoming more common. For example, in 1997 Apple Computers was identified as being among the 10 poor performers. 'Apple's top management lack experience in the personal computer field.' And CalPERS stated that it was 'dissatisfied with the high salaries paid to management in the light of poor performance'. CalPERS voted against Apple's board at its shareholder meeting. Reebok International was also identified as being a poor performer. In particular, CalPERS was concerned 'that Reebok's management has operated with insufficient accountability to the board'.

BA, 2000

Standard Life Investments, which had a 2.3 per cent stake in BA, threatened to vote against acceptance of the company report and accounts in protest at the compensation package being given to Robert Ayling, the former CEO. At the AGM in July 2000, BA's chairman, Lord Marshall, pledged to review the procedure in awarding the controversial £1.98 million pay-off and a £260,000-a-year pension to Ayling. He stated that the board would review its process in reaching the settlement 'to see what lessons could be learnt for the future and to satisfy itself that there is nothing further that should be done in respect of that settlement'.

Investor Opinion Survey Results, 2000

In June 2000, the management consultants McKinsey and Co published their investor opinion survey on corporate governance to discover how institutional investors perceive and value corporate governance in both developed and emerging countries. The survey gathered responses from over 200 institutional investors who together manage $3.25 trillion assets. Key findings included:

▌ Three-quarters of institutional investors say board practices are at least as important to them as financial performance when they are evaluating companies for investment. In Latin America almost half the respondents consider board practices to be more important than financial performance.

▌ Over 80 per cent of institutional investors say they would pay more for the shares of a well-governed company than for those of a poorly governed company with comparable financial performance.

▌ The actual premium institutional investors say that they would be willing to pay for a well-governed company differs by country. For example, institutional investors say they would pay 18 per cent more for the shares of a well-governed company in the UK than for the shares of a company with a similar financial performance but poorer governance practices. They would be willing to pay a 22 per cent premium for a well-governed Italian company and a 27 per cent premium for one in Venezuela or Indonesia.

International stock exchanges

Growing transparency of board decision processes is also of importance to the listings directors of stock exchanges. As the global flow of capital increases so stock exchanges must compete for listings. Listings directors are reasserting the key corporate governance values of:

▌ accountability;

▌ probity;

▌ transparency.

When mixed with the newly forming global standards of finance, banking, civil law and corporate governance, this will be an increasingly powerful force for good. International stock exchanges now require higher levels of investment protection through good corporate governance. This will attract more international capital to them.

The Combined Code (1998)

The Combined Code (1998) has identified principles of corporate governance for listed companies in the UK. The principles cover: 1) companies – directors, directors' remuneration, relations with shareholders, accountability and audit; and 2) institutional shareholders. The six principles associated with directors are:

1. Every listed company should be headed by an effective board, which should lead and control the company.

2. There are two key tasks at the top of every public company – the running of the board and the executive responsibility for the running of the company's business. There should be a clear division of responsibilities at the head of the company, which will ensure a balance of power and authority so that no one individual has unfettered powers of decision.

3. The board should include a balance of executive and non-executive directors (including independent non-executive directors) such that no individual or small group of individuals can dominate the board's decision taking.

4. The board should be supplied in a timely manner with information in a form and of a quality appropriate to enable it to discharge its duties.

5. There should be a formal and transparent procedure for the appointment of new directors to the board.

6. All directors should be required to submit themselves for re-election at regular intervals and at least every three years.

In addition, the Organization for Economic Cooperation and Development (OECD) and Commonwealth Association of Corporate Governance have both published principles of corporate governance (see appendices 4 and 5 for details).

Employees

The Public Interest Disclosure Act 1998 allows disclosure of any information that tends in the reasonable opinion of the employee to show a relevant failure. Such a failure might be:

▪ that a criminal offence has been, is being or is likely to be committed;

▪ that a miscarriage of justice has occurred, is occurring or is likely to occur;

▪ that someone has failed, is failing or is likely to fail to comply with a legal obligation to which he or she is subject;

▪ that the health and safety of any individual has been, is being or is likely to be endangered;

▪ that the environment has been, is being or is likely to be damaged;

▪ that information relating to any of the above has been, is being or is likely to be concealed.

Some organizations have gone beyond the requirements of this legislation and encourage and even reward whistle blowing.

Abbey National, 1997

In November 1997 Abbey National paid £25,000 reward to a former employee for blowing the whistle on the bank's marketing services director who was jailed for eight years for his part in a £1 million fraud. Mr Brown was working as a sales promotion manager under Mr Doyle when he complained in 1994 about not being consulted about payments to some suppliers. Internal auditors found that Mr Doyle had been receiving bribes for putting through false invoices. In 1995 Mr Brown had to take another job while the trial was pending. This case was the first time that a leading UK company has tangibly rewarded a whistle blower rather than just compensating him or her for losses. Lord Tugendhat, the chairman, wrote a letter to Mr Brown stating that his behaviour was a model to the company.

Pressure groups

Pressure groups such as environmental and human rights groups can also have a significant effect on the board's thinking.

Huntingdon Life, 2000

In April 2000 some of the 1,700 shareholders were targeted by protestors at their homes by the British Union for the Abolition of Vivisection Reform Group. At around the same time:

▌ The Royal Bank of Scotland withdrew a £20 million overdraft from Huntingdon Life, the controversial animal testing laboratory, after bank staff were threatened by animal rights protestors in June 2000.

▌ The company's brokers West LB Panmure also severed ties with the laboratory.

▌ The Labour Party's staff pension fund ordered its fund managers Phillips and Drew to withdraw its holdings in Huntingdon Life. Up until February 2000 it had had an 11 per cent stake in the company.

Tomkins, 2000

Tomkins is best known in the UK for owning companies making cakes (Mr Kipling's), bread (Mother's Pride), jam (Robertson's) and curry products (Sharwood's). They also own Smith and Wesson, a gun company, which accounts for 1 per cent of Tomkins' turnover. It has been reported that because of the growth in ethical investment by the financial institutions Tomkins would like to divest itself of Smith and Wesson. However, this is easier said than done, since S&W has become embroiled in litigation in the United States that could cost millions, and the chance of finding a buyer willing to assume the enormous litigation costs is extremely low. The litigation centres upon manufacturers' third-party liability. It is argued that the company has negligently failed to take advantage of technology to enhance safety, eg triggers that recognize fingerprints, and that the manufacturers' distribution and marketing encourage the wrong sort of people to get their hands on guns.

Ed Schultz, president and CEO of S&W, stated: 'In 1992 when I told somebody I was president and CEO of S&W they were tremendously impressed. Today folks look at me as if I'm some sort of person that goes and delivers terrible dark things. I'm depicted as a gun runner or as a trafficker in bad things.'

S&W has broken ranks with other gun companies and taken the commercial decision to agree to several improvements on product safety and distribution. The implications of this decision have been:

▌ Several cities have dropped S&W from their litigation.

▌ Thirty cities and the federal government have agreed to prefer the company's products.

▌ The Gun Owners of America have urged a boycott of S&W products.

▌ One of the largest US wholesalers has decided not to stock S&W's products.

Shell, 2000

In 1995, Shell decided to dispose of its Brent Spar oil rig in the Atlantic. In the same year the company failed to oppose the Nigerian Government's execution of Ken Saro-Wiwa, a human rights activist in a part of Nigeria where Shell had extensive operations. Robin Aram, Head of Policy Development, was reported as saying, 'We weren't confident that there would be no long-term impact, given the growing interest of the investment community in these softer issues. There was a sense of deep discomfort from our own people' (*Economist*, 22 April 2000: 83). Since 1995 Shell has:

▌ rewritten its business principles;

▌ created systems to implement and monitor the application of these principles;

▌ improved its working relationships with non-governmental organizations (NGOs).

The pooling of information about a company through Web sites and bulletin boards on the Internet taps into a global database and allows both the general public and employee whistle blowers to contribute in relative anonymity. It gives smaller shareholders great leverage and this is likely to grow in the future. Aggrieved customers have also started Web sites to broadcast their anger with companies, banks being a particular target. 'Companies will find this kind of direct action particularly wounding if they have no website of their own – www.badcustomerservice.co.uk has already received more than 20,000 hits. When a browser types the keyword into a search engine, the negative site will be brought up and some people may even initially mistake the vigilante sites for the official one' (Stuart, 2000).

Different countries have different and contradictory attitudes to business corruption. At the one extreme you have, in the Unites States, the Foreign Corrupt Practices Act that can jail US executives for paying bribes overseas. On the other hand there are several European countries in which bribes paid abroad are tax-deductible.

CORPORATE SOCIAL RESPONSIBILITY (CSR)

CSR involves an organization in defining its responsibility to society and subsequently operating its activities within CSR parameters. Some organizations apply CSR to their entire operation, while others adopt policies, variously called 'ethical' or 'green', to parts of their work.

BP, 2000

In 2000, BP rebranded itself with a new flowerhead-shaped logo and stated BP stood for 'beyond petroleum'. The company planned to spend £100 million over the following 12 months with a make-over for its petrol stations and a media advertising blitz. BP claimed that the repositioning reflected the growing interest in cleaner, more environmentally friendly fuels such as natural gas and solar power. BP is a major gas producer and has become a world leader in the development of solar power. Cynics argue that 'beyond petroleum' means that no one knows what BP now stands for and that diversification out of the core business into activities such as office cleaning and supermarkets may occur.

For many years the Co-operative Bank made its ethical policy the platform for its entire business. After reading the policy you might consider how far along these lines your board could or should take your company.

The Co-operative Bank's Ethical Policy

Following extensive consultation with our customers, with regard to how their money should and should not be invested, the Bank's position is that:

▌ It will not invest in or supply financial services to any regime or organisation which oppresses the human spirit, takes away the rights of individuals or manufactures any instrument of torture.

▌ It will not finance or in any way facilitate the manufacture or sale of weapons to any country which has an oppressive regime.

▎ It will actively seek and support the business of organisations which promote the concept of 'Fair Trade', ie trade which regards the welfare and interest of local communities.

▎ It will encourage business customers to take a proactive stance on the environmental impact of their own activities, and will invest in companies and organisations that avoid repeated damage of the environment.

▎ It will actively seek out individuals, commercial enterprises and non-commercial organisations which have a complementary ethical stance.

▎ It will welcome suppliers whose activities are compatible with its Ethical Policy.

▎ It will not speculate against the pound using either its own money or that of its customers. It believes it is inappropriate for a British clearing bank to speculate against the British currency and the British economy using deposits provided by their British customers and at the expense of the British taxpayer.

▎ It will try to ensure its financial services are not exploited for the purposes of money laundering, drug trafficking or tax evasion by the continued application and development of its successful internal monitoring and control procedures.

▎ It will not provide financial services to tobacco product manufacturers.

▎ It will not invest in any business involved in animal experimentation for cosmetic purposes.

▎ It will not support any person or company using exploitative factory farming methods.

▎ It will not engage in business with any farm or other organisation engaged in the production of animal fur.

▎ It will not support any organisation involved in blood sports, which involve the use of animals or birds to catch, fight or kill each other; for example fox hunting and hare coursing.

In addition, there may be occasions when the Bank makes decisions on specific business, involving ethical issues not included in this policy. We will regularly re-appraise customers' views on these and other issues and develop our ethical stance accordingly.

This statement was followed in 1996 by an ecological mission statement, which acknowledges that all areas of human activity, including business, are dependent on the natural world for their well-being.

The Co-operative Bank's Ecological Mission Statement

We, The Co-operative Bank, will continue to develop our business, taking into account the impact our activities have on the environment and society at large. The nature of our activities are such that our indirect impact, by being selective in terms of the provision of finance and banking arrangements, is more ecologically significant than the direct impact of our trading operations.

However, we undertake to continually assess all our activities and implement a programme of ecological improvement based on the pursuit of the following four scientific principles:

1. Nature cannot withstand a progressive build-up of waste derived from the Earth's crust.

2. Nature cannot withstand a progressive build-up of society's waste, particularly artificial persistent substances which it cannot degrade into harmless materials.

3. The productive area of nature must not be diminished in quality (diversity) or quantity (volume) and must be enabled to grow.

4. Society must utilise energy and resources in a sustainable, equitable and efficient manner.

We consider that the pursuit of these principles constitutes a path of ecological excellence and will secure future prosperity for society by sustainable economic activity.

The Co-operative Bank will not only pursue the above path itself, but endeavour to help and encourage all its Partners to do likewise.

We will aim to achieve this by:

▮ Financial Services
Encouraging business customers to take a proactive stance on the environmental impact of their own activities, and investing in companies and organisations that avoid repeated damage of the environment (as stated in our Ethical Policy).

▮ Management Systems
Assessing our ecological impact, setting ourselves clear targets, formulating an action plan and monitoring how we meet them, and publishing the results.

▮ Purchasing Outsourcing
Welcoming suppliers whose activities are compatible with both our Ethical Policy and Ecological Mission Statement, and working in partnership with them to improve our collective performance.

▌ Support
   Supporting ecological projects and developing partnerships with businesses and organisations whose direct and indirect output contributes to a sustainable society.

▌ Legislation
   Adhering to environmental laws, directives and guidelines while continually improving upon our own contribution to a sustainable society.

McDonald's, 2000

The fast-food chain McDonald's had a poor corporate social responsibility reputation in the UK where it employed 70,000 people. In the late 1990s, McDonald's sued two environmentalists for libelling the company. The so-called 'McLibel case' lasted over two and a half years and was the longest libel trial in UK history. A McDonald's outlet was attacked in the anti-capitalist riots in London in 1999. In 2000, demonstrators targeted another branch. McSpotlight is an anti-McDonald's Web site, which accuses the company of cruelty to animals, damage to the environment and exploitation of workers.

In 2000, McDonald's decided to work with the demonstrators as a result of these campaigns. It held meetings with the animal welfare group Compassion in World Farming and as a result 90 per cent of eggs used by McDonald's in the UK are now free-range.

Many organizations choose to become involved in community and charitable activities. For example, the community and charitable support given by Dearle and Henderson (see Chapter 9, Case 3) includes: kit for an under-13s boys football team, an annual dinner of a housing trust, a senior citizens' Christmas lunch, the national annual Housing Action Trust conference and the Royal Hospital for Neuro-disability.

AVOIDANCE OF SCANDAL AND BEING IN THE PUBLIC EYE

If your company is to survive and prosper in the 21st century, it needs to be properly and professionally directed. Over the last two decades there have been many examples of companies that have failed to survive because of ineffective board leadership. This includes:

▌ Robert Maxwell's pillage of his companies' pension funds in 1991;

▌ the failure of the BCCI bank through reckless lending totalling several billion pounds in 1991;

▌ the liquidation in 1989 of British and Commonwealth despite having had a market value of nearly £2 billion in 1987;

▌ the collapse of Barings Bank through lax trading procedures in Singapore and London in 1996;

▌ Polly Peck's slide from a market value of £1.75 billion to a deficit of nearly £400 million within one month in the early 1990s with an alleged £1.3 billion fraud.

In 1999–2000 there was extensive press coverage over shake-ups on the boards of the BBC, British Airways, Sainsbury's and Marks and Spencer. NatWest was taken over by the Royal Bank of Scotland after a very hostile and well-publicized battle. Tomkins was another example when in October 2000, Greg Hutchings resigned as chief executive. The annual accounts of Tomkins in the previous accounting year had made no mention of four corporate aircraft, one helicopter, two company flats and a wife and housekeeper on the payroll. The issues resulting from these collapses and shake-ups have given rise to increased interest in corporate governance and board development issues by a number of stakeholder groups.

General public

The publicity given to scandals revealed to the general public that their personal investments, savings and pensions were far more vulnerable than they had realized. In addition, the increase in subsequent re-dundancies and unemployment caused them to throw off the comfy assumptions that boards must know what they are doing. Increasingly, people started asking if boards were competent and showed by their actions that they were worried by the vague answers.

If you're a director of a small firm your 'public' may be quite local. But it might become quite vociferous if any misdeeds by a member of your board were publicized by a campaigning local newspaper. What procedures do you have in place to handle such a situation – not to deny it, of course, but to seek the best possible outcome for the company and its stakeholders? If you're a director of a large firm your 'public' may be vast. In this case, it is critical that you have procedures in place.

Politicians

Politicians are becoming increasingly keen to assuage public concern when disquiet leads to the cry that something needs to be done. Such pressures are likely to grow as board incompetence in an increasingly turbulent world is exposed more frequently and more publicly. The board's attitude to probity, accountability and transparency in these situations is critical.

British Nuclear Fuels, 1999

As a result of an internal quality control audit in 1999, BNFL admitted falsifying quality checks on mixed oxide fuel manufactured at Sellafield. Checks revealed that quality control data for the fuel had been falsified because workers considered the task of measuring pellets to be uncomfortable and unimportant. In February 2000, the Nuclear Installations Inspectorate identified a 'treacle layer' of middle managers who had not adopted quality control practices, and 'systematic management failures'. As a result of the report:

▪ Kansai Electric Power of Japan banned BNFL from bidding for further contracts (January 2000).

▪ John Taylor quit as CEO (February 2000).

▪ Germany banned shipments of BNFL fuel (March 2000).

▪ The US Energy Secretary reviewed all work carried out by BNFL for the US Government (March 2000).

▪ The UK Government postponed plans to privatize up to 49 per cent of BNFL (March 2000).

▪ The BNFL chairman announced the departure of the finance director and all six non-executive directors (April 2000).

IF DEVELOPMENT IS SO IMPORTANT, HOW DO YOU MAKE IT HAPPEN?

Most directors are aware that very little development takes place at board level. The main reason may simply be that they don't think they need it. After all, they may argue, you only train someone when you've carried out a training needs analysis and found a deficiency to be put right. No deficiency, no training, right?

So, if you have a heart attack, will you be happy to be treated by a consultant who qualified 25 years ago and has had no further professional development? Does your accountant adopt a 'seen it all before' attitude after the Budget or produce an update on the effect of the annual blue book on the company? Is your company's Web site written in HTML or XML?

You will, no doubt, have realized from these examples that development is a continuous process. Every new day presents you and the board with new problems. To handle them you need to gain new skills and competencies, to learn, to adapt and to grow.

Let's look at the reasons given by directors for not developing themselves, and offer ways in which the argument can be countered. Typical reasons include:

▮ *Lack of time.* The simple time management procedure of documenting how time is spent will soon reveal time available, but this time must then be committed to a specific development activity. If you refer to the needs analysis in the Securicor case (Chapter 9, Case 1) you will see that time and focus are essential to succeed. And if you don't have some success, you'll give up.

▮ *Lack of money/budget.* An analysis of the cost of not developing usually reveals that development is an investment not a net cost. You must also have enough resources to ensure you get some success from your investment.

▮ *This does not apply to me.* Perhaps you should reread Chapters 1 and 2.

▮ *This does not apply to my board.* Perhaps you should do the analysis of your board recommended in Chapter 1, and reread Chapter 2.

■ *This does not apply to my company.* Your company could well be highlighted in the next edition of this book.

■ *No link between performance and reward.* In several of the case studies you will see that director development was far more effective when it became part of performance and reward. The board should establish the link.

■ *No role models.* The board members should see themselves as role models for managers and the rest of the employees.

■ *No comparator companies.* This argument applies to benchmarking but not to the basic issue of the need for personal and board development.

■ *No champions at a senior level, ie chairman or managing director.* This is a significant argument and indicates that the most senior members of the board have yet to grasp the nettle of their personal need for development. This can be countered by the chairman appointing a personal mentor (more of which later) and embarking on a well-publicized programme of development.

■ *HR not at high enough profile, ie not at board level.* Human resource management and/or development is a company function, but we are discussing the personal responsibility of each member of the board for his or her personal professional development, for which senior HR personnel (or external consultants at a price) can offer advice and guidance.

■ *Ignorance of what is possible.* 'I didn't know that I didn't know.' Our purpose with this book is to help make people aware. And awareness is the first step towards learning. The board has collective responsibility, and any member of the board can help the others to become aware.

■ *Ignorance of consequences.* The chairman might put a regular item on the board agenda to surface the consequences of the members of the board developing and not developing, and the latter should include being voted off.

▌ *Negative board culture, eg autocratic.* Increased interpersonal skills among the members may lead to inroads into the style of board leadership but even autocratic boards can order members to take part in development activities.

▌ *Fear of training.* This is real and has to be handled with sensitivity so that members do not lose face and are not shown up in a negative light before subordinates – coaching and mentoring are two routes forward. And development at the director level *is* different. You're supposed to know everything already, right? Refer to the case studies (see Chapter 9), where you will see company directors go from resistance through scepticism to wanting their own personal development.

Now it's time to take action.

SUMMARY

The key forces driving director and board development are: 1) the superior organization performance and sharper competitive edge that are expected to be the result; and 2) the desire of directors to be more professional in the performance of their duties. In particular, directors have a desire to keep out of jail (legal compliance), avoid scandals and meet stakeholders' expectations.

4

Organization learning and development

As you've already seen, both director and board development need to be firmly anchored to business performance and requirements. In this chapter you will see that, to be effective, they must also be embedded in the culture and vision of the organization. This approach will help to ensure that learning and development are maintained and kept on course even when business pressures mount and priorities change. We shall first consider organization learning and development, and in the following chapters deal with detailed techniques of board development and individual development.

THE LEARNING ORGANIZATION

Bob Garratt developed the concept of a learning organization in the 1980s. Garratt recognized that learning processes were central to the survival and growth of all organizations. He identified two types of organizational learning: strategic learning and policy learning.

Strategic learning

Strategic learning requires that directors get into intellectual helicopter mode to rise above the day-to-day problems. The directors should search for patterns in the changing external environment that allow them to understand the changing competitive pressures. They must also ensure that they have the organizational capabilities to handle these pressures and to create, if necessary, new assets, especially intellectual property rights. Strategic learning is about:

▮ monitoring the changing external world;

▮ reviewing the organization's position in these changes;

▮ making risk assessments to protect and develop enterprise;

▮ broadly deploying the organization's scarce resources to achieve its purpose;

▮ ensuring that there are feedback procedures in place to measure the effectiveness of any strategy being implemented.

Policy learning

Policy learning has two main elements: 1) processes for maintaining and developing the energy and emotional climate of the organization so that its people are committed to it and are willing to learn with it; and 2) processes for monitoring and sensing continuously the organization's changing external environment. Unless an organization can cope with its rapidly changing external environment it will not survive. The board is ultimately responsible for ensuring a sufficient rate of learning in the organization:

> *The need for understanding how organisations learn and accelerate that learning is greater today than ever before. The old days when a Henry Ford, Alfred Sloan or Tom Watson learned for the organisation are gone. In an increasingly dynamic, independent and unpredictable world, it is simply no longer possible for anyone to figure it all out at the top. The*

old model 'the top thinks and the local acts' must now give way to integrative thinking and acting at all levels.

(Senge, 1998: 586)

The directors alone, then, cannot 'learn' for the whole organization. They have to enable the organization to do so. Garratt identified five conditions for increasing the learning capability of the organization:

1. a clear and unique strategy- and policy-formulating role for the board;

2. time and space for the board to think and learn about their strategic role – linking the changing external environment to the dynamics of their internal organizational reality;

3. the creation of a board that values and uses the individually developed strengths of each member through the careful assessment and development of these;

4. delegation of problem-solving and puzzle-solving authority to those on the operational side;

5. a willingness to accept that learning occurs continuously at all levels in the organization so it is the responsibility of directors to create a climate in which it flows freely to where it is needed.

To achieve these conditions in a traditional organization you may have to bring about changes to unblock it.

After a major event – a product failing, a wild business breakthrough, a downsizing crisis or a merger, many companies seem to stumble along, oblivious to the lessons of the past. Mistakes get repeated... Most important, the old ways of thinking that led to the mistakes are never discussed, which often means that they are still in place to spawn new mishaps again and again. Ask individuals about those major events, however, and they often will tell you that they understand exactly what went wrong (or right). Each point of view represents a valid, but limited piece of the solution to the puzzle. If all these perspectives could be integrated coherently, the organisation as a whole might learn what happened, and what to do next. Yet those insights are rarely shared openly. And they are rarely analysed, debated and ultimately internalised by the whole organisation even less frequently. In other words in corporate life even where experience is a good teacher it's still only a private tutor. People in organisations act collectively but they learn individually. That is the central tenet and frustration of organisational learning today.

(Kleiner and Roth, 1997)

In a learning organisation, leaders' roles differ dramatically from that of charismatic decision maker. Leaders are designers, teachers and stewards. These roles require new skills: the ability to build shared vision, to bring to the surface and challenge prevailing mental models and to foster more systemic types of thinking. In short, leaders in learning organisations are responsible for building organisations where people are continually expanding their capabilities to shape their future.

(Senge, 1998: 587)

TECHNIQUES FOR ORGANIZATION LEARNING AND DEVELOPMENT

Analysing the environment

As a start you need to be aware of the macro-dynamics – the large-scale sweeping changes – of your organization's business environment. This awareness will enable the board to give effective direction on how it will achieve its purpose. Such clarity will give everyone in the learning organization the chance to contribute to the policy and gain a sustainable advantage over its competitors.

One relatively simple, but very useful, technique is PPESTT analysis.

Political, physical, economic, social, technological and trade (PPESTT) analysis

As a director you need to make sense of patterns in the fast-changing external environment. With PPESTT analysis you consider political, physical, economic, social, technological and trade issues. The stages of the analysis are:

1. Carry out a brainstorming exercise to create an unsorted list of issues.

2. Discard the irrelevant items and allocate the rest to the PPESTT categories.

3. Tabulate them against their predicted impact on the organization.

4. Keep just the two or three key organizational issues under each heading to be considered for further reflection, action and feedback.

During the exercise you need not be limited by the categories or boundaries, as many topics span more than one; unemployment, for example, may be both a social and an economic influence. It does not matter in which box you put it, so long as you identify it. Table 4.1 shows PPESTT analysis features.

PPESTT analysis may involve:

▌ competitor intelligence;

▌ historical analysis of trends;

▌ external benchmarking (either industrial comparative analysis or best practice comparison);

▌ satisfaction indices for customers, staff, suppliers and the community;

▌ Web sites and e-commerce feedback.

PPESTT is crude but simple. There have been several research projects on whether such broad environmental scanning actually improves an organization's performance. Most support the notion that it does.

Analysis of the competitive environment

Having considered the broad environmental issues, you can now turn to the forces that shape the immediate structure of your organization. Likely forces identified by Porter (1980) include:

▌ *The threat of entry into the industry.* The UK vacuum cleaner industry had been relatively cosy until James Dyson developed a 'bagless' cleaner, failed to get any established company to adopt his idea, set up his own manufacturing facility in 1993 and within three years was outselling his nearest competitor by more than five to one.

Table 4.1 _PPESTT analysis features_

Category	Features monitored
Political Environment	The broad policies and actions of the main political parties in the countries in which you operate. Political changes and forthcoming elections.
Physical Environment	National and global debates on pollution. New or proposed environment regulations.
Economic Environment	Regional, national and international economies. The likely consequences of political rhetoric and behaviour to build alliances where necessary.
Social Environment	Demographic trends in the countries in which you operate. The lifestyle trends amongst your customers. Fast changing fashion trends. New social groupings.
Technological Environment	The evolution of new technologies. Debates on the likely consequences of such development. New market segments.
Trade Environment	Regional, national and international trends. International trade trends between the global blocs. The World Trade Organization decisions to help predict changes in demand.

▌ *The bargaining power of suppliers.* By controlling the quantity of new diamonds entering the market, diamond suppliers (such as De Beers) are able to exert great control over the market price of diamonds.

▌ *The bargaining power of buyers.* In 1999 Ford and General Motors set up an embryo worldwide e-commerce purchasing system for all motor manufacturers, which will have the undoubted effect of increasing commercial pressure on suppliers.

▌ *The threat of substitutes.* Information storage: paintings on cave walls, tablets of stone, papyrus, paper, silk, punch tape, cassette tape, floppy disks, hard disks, CD ROM, DVD, solid state electronics – and chemical or biological formulations next?

▌ *The extent of competitive rivalry.* The level of competition in the chemical industry in the 1990s intensified because of declining demand for chemicals, overcapacity, rising costs and commoditization of the product.

In addition, you may find it useful to consider your organization's competitive position in terms of:

▌ *Product diversity.* Are your products too narrowly focused in a single market to be safe, nicely balanced or too widely spread for your board to direct effectively?

▌ *Geographic coverage.* Have you expanded into markets abroad that you can manage effectively or are you overstretched? Have the markets fulfilled your expectations?

▌ *Number of market segments.* How numerous and clearly defined are the market segments that your organization operates in?

▌ *Distribution channels.* What impact is the Internet likely to have upon your company's distribution channels?

Vauxhall, 1999

In October 1999 Vauxhall announced plans to sell cars directly to customers via the Internet. Vauxhall developed six dot.com models with different specifications from showroom models to avoid direct price comparisons with dealer prices.

Ford, 2000

In August 2000, Ford announced an Internet car purchase system in the United States, which would be run in conjunction with dealers who would in effect take over an order placed from their territory and handle the physical side of the sourcing and delivery.

■ *Branding.* How do your customers value your brand? What resources does your organization spend to protect and increase this value?

■ *Marketing effort.* How does your organization measure customer satisfaction and key customer retention?

■ *Vertical integration.* Is there any threat of companies from further down or up the supply chain providing similar goods or services to the ones your organization provides?

■ *Quality of product or service.* How does your organization measure quality and how does it monitor and improve the quality of its products and services?

Mitsubishi, 2000

In the summer of 2000, Mitsubishi recalled a total of 620,000 vehicles after it was revealed that the company had concealed potentially serious faults for more than 30 years. Senior executives had been aware of the problem but had failed to do anything about it.

■ *R & D capability, cost position and utilization of capacity.* How does your organization compare in these areas with the other organizations within the same industry?

Analysing internal resources and competencies

Internal analysis is the process you use to understand your organization's strategic capabilities and to know what resources you have, how they are balanced and the interrelationships between them.

The resource audit

The resource audit is little more than an exact list of the resources you have in the organization, where they are and what condition they are in. You can usually classify the resources into four types:

1. physical resources – the numbers of machines or their capacity, together with information on their age, condition, capability, location and likely obsolescence;

2. human resources – numbers, range and types of skills, adaptability, willingness to learn, mobility;

3. financial resources – skill at obtaining capital, managing cash, control of debtors and creditors, managing relationships with suppliers of finance;

4. intangibles – these may be easily overlooked – intellectual property, goodwill, a motivated workforce.

Table 4.2 *SWOT analysis*

Issue	Implication
Strengths	Competitively priced service.
	Expertise in niche markets.
	Need to keep costs down.
	A good reputation in niche markets.
Weaknesses	Poor location.
	Weak marketing skills.
	Low visibility.
Opportunities	Increase in small businesses.
	New office units available.
	Businesses need financial help.
	Need to consider leasing arrangements.
Threats	Large firms cutting fees.
	Business rates increasing.
	Need to counter erosion of customer base.
	Need to reconsider location.

Focusing on these four areas within each of the value activities provides a way of breaking down the complexity of an organization.

Strengths, weaknesses, opportunities and threats (SWOT) analysis

SWOT analysis is a framework for examining the strengths, weaknesses, opportunities and threats. A well-executed SWOT will provide you with a clear statement of the current strategic position of the organization. The process is similar to PPESTT analysis: brainstorming, sorting and prioritizing, assessing impact and identifying the major issues for action. In Table 4.2 you can see a worked example of this for a small accountancy practice.

Issue-led development

Instead of using SWOT analysis, some boards use issue-led techniques. In this case the board considers the key issues facing the business. An example of an issue-led approach is given by Luke March, former director of corporate governance at BT:

Issues for Board focus at BT include:

- *Strategic*

- *Developmental*

- *International*

- *Grow shareholder value*

- *Oversight and control.*

(March, 1999)

Your board might place each of these on a series of agendas, or arrange special meetings to tackle the items one at a time. The topic 'shareholder value' should generate a deep and lively debate in the board of every company, no matter the size. In a learning organization, the board debates should be followed (or even preceded) by further debates and analyses at every level.

Learning histories

A new method for developing collective reflection is the construction of a learning history. This is a written narrative of a company's recent critical episodes, for example merger, acquisition, new product development, new market development and downsizing. The learning history is often a document of 20 to 100 pages. Each page is divided into two columns: the left-hand column describes the relevant event with direct quotations from the relevant people involved, and the right-hand column contains the analysis and interpretation, and commentary by outsiders such as consultants and academics who specialize in organizational learning and development.

Groups can then be set up to use the learning history as a basis for discussion. By reflecting together on the issues, they might gain a better understanding of them and improve their ability to handle such issues in the future.

One recurring lesson [of using learning histories] is that 'hard' results such as financial returns or technical objectives are frequently a function of 'soft' issues such as a company's culture. Indeed the learning histories written to date have shown that in re-engineering, redesign or other change initiatives, the most critical factor for success is the quality of human interaction in the organisation.

(Kleiner and Roth, 1997: 177)

Investors in People

Some organizations have used the Investors in People (IIP) framework to assess the effectiveness of their training and development processes. The IIP performance indicators are listed in Appendix 7.

Developing a vision

You and your fellow directors may already have a vision of what you want your business to become. A vision is a clear view of the future state that the organization will ideally attain. An inspirational vision is always intangible and frequently open-ended in its nature.

▮ Motorola have a vision of a wireless world where everyone has a lifelong personal telephone number and a portable phone.

▮ Microsoft has a vision of a personal computer on every desk in every house.

▮ Apple has a vision of a computer for every man, woman and child.

To convey your vision to senior management you may prepare a mission statement, together with a strategic plan, to express what needs to be done to reach the envisioned state.

Designing a process to develop a strategic plan

Once directors have employed their strategic thinking and crystallized their vision for the organization, they should produce a set of documented plans suitable for communication to interested parties. The plans are likely to be at three levels of strategy:

1. at the corporate or company-wide level where the overwhelming concern is: what sort of business should we be in?

2. at the business level where the main question is: how do we establish and sustain competitive advantage in this particular business?

3. at the functional level where the main focus is: how do we maximize the productivity of our resources, be it human resources, marketing resources, financial resources, etc?

We can illustrate this last point with an example of a marketing strategy that would:

■ establish marketing objectives such as market share;

■ formulate strategies for attaining these objectives, such as media expenditure or point-of-sale promotion;

■ lay down plans that cover the utilization and acquisition of marketing resources.

So, the marketing strategy would answer the following questions:

■ What is the current competitive position of the company within its chosen markets?

■ What changes in marketing objectives are required to fulfil the overall business strategy?

▍ What strategies in the marketing field will enable the business to meet the objectives?

▍ What needs to be changed in the total marketing resources or in their utilization?

In broad terms, then, your marketing strategy should aim to align the internal marketing effort with both the external environment and the overall business strategy. The issues you identify at this stage should be turned into medium- or long-term plans. Lower down the hierarchy you will need operational plans. The sales force, for example, will need to know what to do next week! So your marketing strategy leads to operational plans that will generate short-term tactical plans. In our example of a point-of-sale campaign, you will need rotas of sales visits by the sales force and monitoring arrangements to make sure their efforts are in line with the overall higher-order strategies.

From this marketing example you should be able to develop your business strategy, functional strategies and tactical plans for all the functional areas of the business. You can see the relationship between the various levels of strategies in Figure 4.1.

SUMMARY

Learning processes are central to the survival and growth of all organizations. The board needs to set out a clear strategy- and policy-formulating role for itself, and devote time and space to thinking about the organization's strategy and policy.

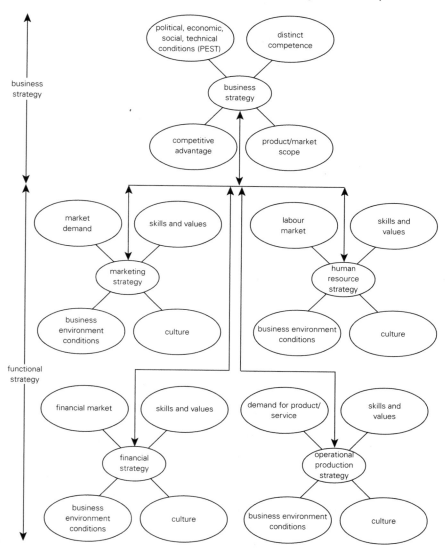

Figure 4.1 *The linkage between business strategy and functional strategies*
(*Source:* Pierce et al, 1997a)

5

Board development

The purpose of the board is to ensure the organization's prosperity by collectively directing the organization's affairs whilst meeting the appropriate interests of its shareholders and relevant stakeholders. A board may be composed of brilliant individuals and yet be ineffective. So, it's not just a matter of bringing together the best brains and waiting for the successful outcomes. A board can only fulfil its true potential if it is properly selected, organized and led. These activities are normally undertaken by the chairman of the board, part of whose role is to manage the board's business and act as its facilitator and guide. This involves the board asking some pertinent questions:

- Is the board performing at its optimum?

- What is the optimum for the board?

- Are standards and goals set?

- How are underperforming boards identified?

- How is spare capacity of a board identified?

- How can spare capacity be utilized more effectively?

▌ How can the capability of the board be measured?

▌ What level of competence should a board have?

▌ How can the board be benchmarked against others?

In this chapter we consider:

▌ board composition and organization;

▌ clarifying the powers, roles and responsibilities of the board;

▌ planning and managing board and board committee meetings;

▌ developing the effective board.

BOARD COMPOSITION AND ORGANIZATION

When building the potential of a board, you can consider a number of strategies to deal with the membership and how they work. You might:

▌ increase the number of executive directors;

▌ increase the number of non-executive directors;

▌ make more use of external resources within the board's networks;

▌ make better use of underutilized resources within the board and company;

▌ increase the capability of the board in areas of strategic thinking;

▌ develop the knowledge and expertise of existing directors;

▌ develop the board by looking especially at processes in use.

In the following action lists you will see a number of tasks that will help lead to improvements in the board's membership and methods. Undertaking these tasks is not a lone job and should be done with like-minded colleagues from the board. Many of the issues will cause conflict, especially where directors have lost touch with current methods and thinking.

Before you start, select your collaborators and carefully think out your strategy. Will it be 'a spanner in the works' or 'softly, softly, catchee monkee'?

Action list:

1. Consider the ratio and number of executive and non-executive directors.

2. Consider the energy, experience, knowledge, skills and personal attributes of current and prospective directors in relation to the future needs of the board as a whole, and develop specifications and processes for new appointments as necessary.

3. Consider the cohesion, dynamic tension and diversity of the board, and its leadership by the chairman.

4. Make and review succession plans for directors and the company secretary.

5. Where necessary, remove incompetent or unsuitable directors or the company secretary, taking relevant legal, contractual, ethical and commercial matters into account.

6. Agree proper procedures for electing a chairman and appointing the managing director and other directors.

7. Identify potential candidates for the board, make selection and agree terms of appointment and remuneration, with all new appointments being agreed by every board member.

8. Provide new board members with a comprehensive induction to board processes and policies, including an introduction to their new role and inclusion within the company.

9. Monitor and appraise rigorously and regularly each individual's performance, behaviour, knowledge, effectiveness and values.

10. Identify development needs and training opportunities for existing and potential directors and the company secretary.

You might well be in a state of shock if you can foresee many problems arising with members of your board, but the best way forward is to grasp the nettle and start with Number 1. You will see some useful examples of board composition issues in the case studies (see Chapter 9).

CLARIFYING THE POWERS, ROLES AND RESPONSIBILITIES OF THE BOARD

Having reviewed the board's composition, you're now in a strong position to look at the board's workings. Does it try to do too much itself? In what ways could its corporate direction processes be more effectively handled?

Action list:

1. Define the powers and roles that the board reserves for itself.

2. Review the relevance of the company's memorandum and articles of association, pertinent legislation and corporate governance guidelines.

3. Specify the powers and roles to be delegated to individual directors, including the chairman.

4. Specify the powers to be delegated to board committees and determine their terms of reference, life span, leadership and membership.

5. Empower the managing director to implement the decisions of the board and other specific matters not reserved to the board itself, and confirm such empowerment by a formal resolution to the board.

PLANNING AND MANAGING BOARD AND BOARD COMMITTEE MEETINGS

At this stage you should review the board's procedures. Even the smallest of family-run businesses will benefit from regularization of what may be a lunchtime chat. This is especially true if the time for succession to the top posts is approaching.

Action list:

1. Establish, maintain and develop reporting and meeting procedures for the board and its committees.

2. Determine policy for the frequency, purpose, conduct and duration of the meetings, and especially the setting of the agenda.

3. Create comprehensive agendas covering all the necessary and appropriate issues through the year while also including important immediate issues.

4. Assign tasks and objectives to individual members, including especially the chairman, managing director, finance director and company secretary, and agree the working relationships between them.

5. Define and review regularly the information needs of the board.

6. Adopt efficient and timely methods for informing and briefing board members prior to the meetings.

7. Maintain proper focus on the board's key role and tasks ensuring that all the major strategic issues affecting the company's visibility, reputation and prosperity are addressed.

8. Allow sufficient time for important matters to be discussed thoroughly.

9. Encourage all directors to attend all board meetings and to contribute appropriately to discussions, drawing on the full range of relevant opinions, knowledge, skills and experience.

10. Draw together the pertinent points from the discussions in a timely way in order to reach well-informed decisions that command consensus.

11. Ensure that adequate minutes are kept and that board attendance and board decisions are properly recorded.

DEVELOPING THE EFFECTIVE BOARD

You may be aware of a definition of board development as: 'The systematic maintenance, improvement and broadening of knowledge, experience and skills and the development of personal qualities of board members helpful in the execution of the role of the board' (IoD, 1999). Board development should be seen as an integral part of the normal work of the board, not as an additional task. It should be owned and managed by the board as a whole. The chairman of the board is likely to play a leading and co-ordinating role in the process.

Board development issues normally arise out of the process of reviewing:

▪ board composition and organization;

▪ board and management responsibilities;

▪ planning and managing board and board committee meetings.

Table 5.1 shows the results of a recent survey of boardroom development issues (IoD, 1998b). The responses are expressed as a percentage of respondents who identified the boardroom development issue as important.

You might well regard these results as quite disappointing, especially the low ratings for updating and appraisal.

Mapping development needs

The IoD Standards for the Board (1999) provide a useful diagnostic framework for improving the effectiveness of a board. Any diagnostic framework relating to developing a board should include the following:

▪ knowledge, skills and understanding;

▪ directors' qualities and attributes;

▪ the board as a working group, including decision-making processes.

Table 5.1 *Boardroom issues*

Boardroom Development Issue	Respondents Who Identified Issue as Important
Strategy development	75%
Leadership	73%
Teamwork	65%
Continual development and updating of knowledge	49%
Continual development and updating of skills	48%
Adaptability and flexibility	46%
Selection	38%
Succession	38%
Appraisal of the board	28%
Appraisal of individual directors	26%
Remuneration of directors	24%
Preparation for board appointment	21%

(*Source*: IoD, 1998b)

In evaluating the framework, the following issues should be addressed:

▪ How should the development needs of each director be addressed?

▪ Should formal or informal development be used?

▪ Have the needs of the board been addressed?

▪ What is the scale of the development challenge; is a major programme needed or are there just gaps to fill?

What to do

There are a number of activities that you can introduce to the board as part of its board development strategy.

Analysis of current board performance

In preparation for a discussion on board performance, ask all your members to:

▌ look through the papers for the past few meetings of your board, especially the agenda and minutes;

▌ answer the following questions:

– To what extent has the board focused upon the key issues that should be the concern of directors?

– How does the board monitor its performance?

Discussions

Development can occur through discussions at board meetings. However, you may find it more effective if you adopt a separate structure. Many companies have used board forums to structure their discussions.

Boardroom forums

In the mid-1990s, the London and Edinburgh Insurance Company set up a boardroom forum to make the firm 'fit for the year 2000'. The forum was made up of the board's strategy group and divisional or business unit heads. External presenters such as academics and main board directors of leading non-competing organizations were invited to address the forum. Topics included: business process re-engineering, sustaining staff loyalty, decentralization, customer loyalty, leadership, innovation and teamworking. David Macmillan, the personnel director, is reported as saying: 'The frank exchange of views during syndicate discussions wouldn't have happened in a more formal business setting'. Benefits arising from the forum included:

▌ the development of a new set of missions and values;

▌ the development of a more open dialogue;

▌ freeing up of directors expressing their opinions and following up on ideas.

(Adapted from Syrett and Lammiman, 1999: 45)

Working parties or task forces

Board members carry out other roles such as membership or chairmanship of board committees, board working parties or task forces set up for specific time-limited purposes.

Mentors

Some long-established members of the board may accept the responsibility of acting as mentors to new members. The role may include inducting them to the board, initiating them into the way the board works and encouraging regular discussion and review of the new member's development. On the other hand, you may find some members prefer to have a director of another, non-competitive organization to undertake this role, since there is the possibility of personal conflict arising from the board's normal activities.

Away days

Large companies have just as many problems as small companies, and large size can often mean lack of team spirit. It could be because the chairman doesn't really know the executive and non-executive directors as people, or because the directors don't understand the strengths of one another's experiences and background. A most effective way of improving interpersonal knowledge is to get the whole group off-site to spend time together in a more relaxed environment where social and business interchange can merge. Away from the day-to-day pressures and interruptions of office life, the focus of sharp minds can develop the strategic business plan or mission statement, or reappraise company goals in a far shorter time.

You must have a specific objective linked to work for an away day. Concentrating on your navel and looking at team processes is not usually good enough.

Experimenting

When the board comes up with a 'good' idea it might be time for a controlled experiment from which everyone can learn. 'I think it is impossible to predict what will happen when you deploy a strategic thought inside an organisation. I don't think you can predict people's behaviour. Therefore, you've got to see how the idea works. You've got to learn how to build something with a bit of a track record, which you can then apply more widely' (Browne, CEO at BP, quoted in Prokesch, 1997: 160).

Use of consultants

You may find that an experienced developer is an effective catalyst for developing the cohesiveness of the whole board. He or she may sit in on board meetings, acting as a constructive critic to the board as a whole, and/or offering individual directors development and guidance as necessary.

There are boards whose directors work so closely together in the day-to-day management of the business that they find difficulty in standing back and considering policy and longer-term strategic issues. This situation applies particularly to smaller companies whose directors often have a significant shareholding and a functional management responsibility.

The chairman may well benefit from the guidance of a suitably qualified and experienced consultant. They might work together to restructure board meetings and agenda items. Such guidance might be extended to schooling the whole board in changing their pattern of behaviour and processes used at board meetings.

The appointment of one or two non-executive directors to the board can be a great help in achieving the right change in emphasis. Suitably experienced, independent and knowledgeable outside directors can help focus attention on essential board issues by their insistence on addressing such matters. High-calibre additions to the board of this type can do wonders in developing an upper-grade management team into a really effective board.

Performance review

For every board member, learning must be linked to performance objectives if it is to lead to changed behaviour and improved performance. Your learning must be based on performance management, with performance objectives agreed and set. These objectives should set out the actions that will lead to a significant improvement in business performance. Some of the agreed actions will require you to make changes to the way that you work – in your behaviour, how you make use of your time, or the different knowledge and expertise you need to acquire. Performance reviews need to be held regularly and cover both the business performance and progress towards making agreed changes.

Peer feedback

You might consider using the approach Bob Garratt describes in the following quotation. Note, however, his references to trust and to the use of a facilitator:

When working with boards I have built up a level of trust through sharing peer feedback – the process is simple. There is a flip chart sheet for every board member with the words stop, start and continue written on it. The participants are then given plenty of time to fill in individually their needs of each other board member specifically to:

▮ *Stop doing things that block their colleagues' ability to work effectively*

▮ *Start doing things that will better use their colleagues' talents and aspirations*

▮ *Continue doing the things that really help their colleagues.*

There is usually a long and quiet period where people read their own sheets and ponder the meaning of them. After that there is an even longer period where they come together to discuss the meaning of the words written, and the emotions expressed, before getting agreement on how they will try to work together in future and how it will be monitored. Again the use of a facilitator is strongly recommended.

(Garratt, 2000a: 121)

Board and director thinking styles

A very different approach to board development has been devised by Bob Garratt (1995) based on pioneering research into effective intelligence (EI) carried out by Jerry Rhodes (1988).

We pointed out earlier that managing is literally a 'hands-on' activity whilst directing is primarily 'brains-on'. Directing is essentially a reflective *intellectual* process where the eyes are scanning the horizon. It is, therefore, less susceptible to quantitative measurement, but is still measurable, especially in qualitative terms.

You and the other directors on your board may see yourselves as fundamentally pragmatic activists. This is because you have probably had an executive career where a 'can do', 'hands-on' approach has been richly rewarded. However, your need is now in directorial competence, especially in strategic thinking. Your key role is to provide independent, diverse, critical *thought*, debate and learning, together with the competence to ensure that the board's risk-assessment and decision-taking processes are as effective as is possible with the people comprising the board. Figure 5.1 illustrates how a learning board can create a review cycle.

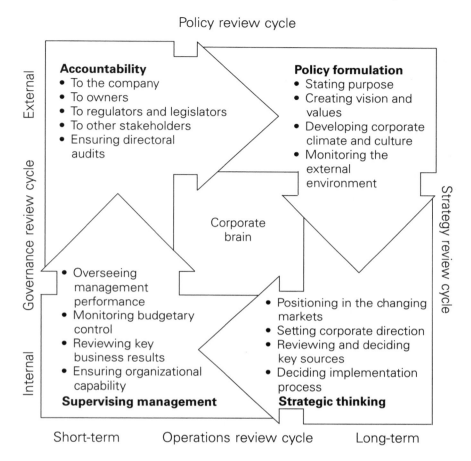

Figure 5.1 *The Learning Board model*

(*Source:* Garratt, 1996)

As we saw in Chapter 1, the board has to balance two building blocks: *conformance* with the externally-imposed legal constraints and its internally-imposed budgets; and *performance* in its rapidly changing external world in applying foresight, assessing risks, taking and implementing strategic decisions successfully, *and* learning from them.

Such a difficult and dynamic balancing act requires the board to have a sufficient range of thinking styles to give direction effectively.

The basic building blocks of effective intelligence

Rhodes' Thinking-Intentions Profile (TIP) is a unique instrument to determine thinking *preferences*. It uses answers to a questionnaire to codify what goes on in a person's brain before behaviour is seen by others, and before personality traits become involved in the micro politics of groups. It deals with three fundamental aspects of the effective intelligence of the mind:

1. **Judgement**: What is right? – this draws on the past: the values and logic which we have learned through nature and nurture.

2. **Information**: What is true? – this focuses on the present and our ability to analyse data, by the use of discriminating questions, to retrieve information to solve our problem.

3. **Imagination**: What is new? – this reaches out into the future and our ability to go beyond the bounds of the immediate and our past to create pictures of possibilities for hopefully better times.

To achieve useful blends of judgement, information and imagination directors need time and money to attend workshops to undergo a learning process. It involves conscious benchmarking, appropriate developmental processes and, later, competency measures for personal feedback.

Aspects of the three effective intelligence building blocks

Each of the three basic building blocks has a 'hard' and 'soft' aspect.

1. Judgement

▌ 'Hard' judgement relies on the use of logic and rationality. A director who scores highly in this area is likely to be seen as highly logical – a 'law-bringer' to complex situations – but, if this strength is overdone, it is likely to kill ideas through the inappropriately early application of the razor edge of logic. (colour-coded hard blue)

▌ 'Soft' judgement relies more on the value systems in which you were brought up – what is 'right and wrong', 'good and bad' in your world. This relies on an internal logic, rather than an espoused external one and, if strong, can lead to passionate commitment to a cause or person. In this form, the director may well be seen by others as a 'missionary'. (colour-coded soft blue)

2. Information

▮ 'Hard' information is exactly that – something that can be seen and measured. It is more the approach of the 'accountant' than that of a director of finance. It depends on metrics and calculation. (colour-coded hard red)

▮ 'Soft' information is very different. It relies on _sensing_ what is occurring. Using all six senses, individuals will feel what is occurring now. They will usually describe their thoughts through feelings – 'I went into that group and it just didn't feel right'; 'I came away from our meeting with a strange taste in my mouth'. This sensing has a lot to do with the participant's perception of the micro politics of a group, especially a board. One could call people who are strong in expressing thoughts through feelings 'poets'. (colour-coded soft red)

3. Imagination

▮ 'Hard' imagination is about realizing what could change. It is to see what might be, and then using ingenuity to get there. This is where the 'strategic engineers', the 'implementers' and the 'fixers' come into play to make future possibilities happen. (colour-coded hard green)

▮ 'Soft' imagination is about seeing the big picture, especially one in the distant future. It is about being visionary – seeing the future sunny uplands or the Elysian Fields to which many aspire. These are the 'visionaries'. (colour-coded soft green)

We are all a mixture of the six styles. We are driven by our high scores and tend to avoid areas with low scores. For a board, individual scores are not critical. The big question is, what pattern of effective intelligence do we have around the boardroom table? Where are our strengths, our overdone strengths and our weaknesses as a group? And will we be capable of effectively deploying them to assure our roles, tasks and accountabilities as directors?

A survey of UK directors' thinking styles

Garratt (1995) surveyed 180 UK directors. The range of industries represented was: Health 18 per cent; Manufacturing 17 per cent; Public

Servants 10 per cent; Retail 8 per cent; Financial 6 per cent; Know-how Services 6 per cent; Others 35 per cent. Of this sample, 80 per cent were male and 20 per cent female.

Garratt had a view of the ideal directorial set of thinking competences. The board would be strong in vision (soft green), ingenuity to roll-out strategy (hard green), good at identifying, benchmarking and using hard data (hard red) and capable of taking sound decisions (hard blue); whilst keeping under control the ability to sense the immediate environment (soft red) and to commit to a course of action (soft blue). However, from his empirical observations, he predicted that the highest scores would be in the EI areas of logic (hard blue), sensing (soft red) with a runner-up of visioning (soft green). He predicted also that the weakest areas by far would be in values and commitment (soft blue) and especially in resourceful ingenuity (hard green) with a runner-up in hard facts (hard red).

The results of the analysis of the survey of 180 directors identified the following preferences (1 indicates the highest preference):

1. 'soft' information (soft red)

2. 'hard' judgement (hard blue)

3. 'soft' judgement (soft blue)

4. 'hard' information (hard red)

5. 'hard' imagination (hard green)

6. 'soft' imagination (soft green)

Rhodes and Garratt then analysed this sample at two levels – the six colour-coded *thinking preferences* (TIP), previously explained, and the 21 specific *thinking-intentions*, 'thunks' for short, which underpin them.
The thunks in each TIP are:

1. *Judgement*: distinguish, compare, test, value, interpret, predict, commit;

2. *Information*: specify, categorize, look in/out, observe, code, set level;

3. *Imagination*: redescribe, challenge, escape, pursue, symbolize, unform, pretend, feel.

This second thunks read-out (figure 5.2) reveals which elements of thinking are ranked low or high *within* a colour, regardless of the overall ranking of the colour scores. Often this presents an apparently contradictory picture. An individual thunk may score high when its associated TIP scores low.

One example highlights this. Vision (soft green) is a vital part of board performance. The TIP results put soft green as the directors' bottom thinking preference, but the soft green thunk 'feel' or intuition had a high ranking. However, the soft green thunk 'pretend', concerned with scenarios and simulation, ranked almost at the bottom. This result squares with empirical observation – directors are often incompetent at generating scenarios in any real imaginative detail – and implies that they need help to develop consciously the diversity of their thinking about the future.

As this example shows, to benchmark and develop a board of directors it is essential to be able to use the effective intelligence data at these two levels of analysis. While the information at the TIP colours level provides a quickly grasped picture of a board's mix of thinking styles, this can obscure vital specifics, which the thunks analysis usefully points up. This is, of course, even more pertinent when it comes to examining individual profiles.

Hard Judgement (hard blue)		Hard Information (hard red)		Hard Imagination (hard green)	
Distinguish	2	Specify	7	Pursue	6
Test	5	Look in/out	12	Challenge	10
Compare	16	Categorize	17	Escape	14
				Redescribe	18
Soft Judgement (soft blue)		Soft Information (soft red)		Soft Imagination (soft green)	
Interpret	1	Code	3	Feel	8
Commit	4	Set level	9	Uniform	13
Predict	15	Observe	11	Pretend	20
Value	19			Symbolize	21

1 = Highest preference   21 = Lowest preference

Figure 5.2 *The rank order of colour-coded thinking-intentions (TIPS) of 180 UK directors*

Luckily this is not the whole picture. When the split is made between the male and female members of the sample, there is an interesting shift. The women are less at risk in the arena of complete and accurate facts and figures than men, and their top ranking of soft red perceptiveness is head and shoulders above the men, accounting for the primacy of this factor overall. But how many women do you have working on your board, and what weight do they carry in shaping the thinking patterns of the group?

Another factor is that within the broad averages some individuals have profiles that are far from any norm. How would your colleagues view them and cope with them? Can the board learn to value this diversity and use it to the board's advantage?

Moreover, there is no universal good profile: the best board profile is the one that is appropriate to the task being faced. Sadly, most boards meet infrequently and, as members do not understand one another's thinking profiles, they fail to draw on any collective strength found in the diversity around the boardroom table. If you can use such diversity, then your board effectiveness should be improved greatly.

The results of the sample of UK directors suggested a dislike of organized information. Yet listed companies must now report annually on their risk-assessment and decision-taking processes under the Turnbull Report requirements. You may need to take action to ensure that your board is intellectually equipped to meet this challenge.

Charting the deeper waters

Strategic business issues are complex because you cannot easily see their structure or their relationships with other issues. Yet it is possible to discern some order in the chaos of complexity and from this to construct 'thought-maps' of the kinds of issue you face. In the EI system, these maps are made of thinking-intentions and the elemental questions to be found in each of them. Such maps differentiate, for example, between the contrasting thinking demands of decision making and strategy, invention and innovation, diagnosis and planning, investigation and persuasion. Because these require different aspects and combinations of thought, they account for people of various profiles feeling either more or less comfortable in different parts of the board discussions.

Asking good discriminating questions is the quintessential tool of superior strategic thinkers. Really effective directors form the questions that matter, even, and especially when, they know very little about the answers to expect. Independent directors in particular operate largely out of ignorance. The best of them turn this to advantage with perceptive, insightful and probing questions that develop consciously the range of their thinking styles and their personal confidence. To achieve this style you may need to extend your personal range beyond the disciplines of your professional specialism and your natural propensities. There is nothing more incisive than a question that drives right to the nub. These maps of questioning are tools that crystallize directorial best practice.

Directors as guardians of thought

Directors are the guardians, not only of the company's assets but also of its opportunities – its strategy for thought and learning. The external future is not knowable and is always unpredictably changing. The main reason for developing thinking skills is so that the board's rate of learning is at least equal to the rate of change in its environment. Yet the elements of our thinking processes are relatively static. Here we can really be in control of what goes on. It is your inner mental strategy and awareness of strengths and weaknesses that steers your approach to external risks.

Your board, then, has to orchestrate its own learning, and the generation and valuing of intellectual capital, as well as encouraging the opportunity for intelligent use of thinking effectiveness throughout your organization. They can quality-assure the company's thinking systems, especially those for dealing with risk based not only on known and extrapolated experience (the hard red, soft red and soft blue) but also the crucial role of imagination (soft and hard green).

You can also set standards for the use of thought by the way you handle proposals for approval. In a real learning organization, there is no need to expect the quality of thinking to be any less the closer you get to those at the coal face, who are more likely to know what they are talking about.

For more information on effective intelligence visit the website at: www.effectiveintelligence.com.

How to introduce board development into an organization

In order to maximize the benefits of board development, you should consider taking the introductory process through a number of stages:

1. *Obtaining buy-in from the chairman and managing director.* The developer has to form a working relationship with the board and especially the chairman and managing director. This is to ensure that the necessary development and learning will become integral to the optimum performance of the board and ultimately the company. Support from the top signals to others in the company that development is an important activity within the organization.

2. *Move to board responsibility for self-development.* After managing director / chairman buy-in, the next stage is to encourage the board to take responsibility for its own growth, as a continuous process. This must be a combination of individual director development and team improvement.

3. *Include board and director development in the business plan, with a budget.* Once the board recognizes the importance of its development as part of the company's strategy and successful operation, it should write it into the annual and long-term business plans, with sufficient budget to make sure it happens effectively.

4. *Get the 'champions' on side.* In any organization there are influential people who can add weight to a strategy or programme and make all the difference to whether it happens or not. You know who they are in your own business. They may be influential because of their title and role, such as the finance director, marketing manager or a risk manager, or they may be influential through sheer interest and strong personality. Either way you need to make sure they are on side with the plan and are supportive.

5. *Identify the drivers and publish the plan internally.* Now it's time to tell the employees how their board is planning its developmental strategy and to make clear which individuals are responsible for driving the process. Support from the top needs to be stated openly and the evidence obvious. This should be in the regular newsletters, training programmes or company notices or videos you might have.

6. *Agree a route map and mark the stages.* It's helpful to divide the plan into stages, each of which has its own actions, time plan and result. This allows checks on progress and helps to ensure that the plan doesn't lose direction. The stages should include the board as a whole and individual director development.

7. *Clear the road-blocks.* Many directors do not examine and question their assumptions. As a result they have a limited set of maps setting their direction. They may erect elaborate defensive road-blocks and create smoke screens that prevent themselves and anyone else from challenging either their actions or their assumptions.

The dilemmas of power

Chris Argyris (1977) examined six US presidents and identified several crucial dilemmas:

▪ how to be strong yet admit the existence of dilemmas;

▪ how to behave openly yet not be controlling;

▪ how to advocate their views and still encourage confrontation;

▪ how to respond effectively to subordinates' anxieties in spite of their own;

▪ how to manage fear yet ask people to overcome their fears and become more open;

▪ how to gain credibility for attempts to change leadership style when they are not comfortable with such a style.

In a new learning system people would advocate their views in ways that would invite confrontation, positions would be stated so that they could be challenged and testing would be done publicly.

Experience shows that there are several barriers to success that come up time and time again, usually as excuses as to why the programme is important but cannot be done just now. Either the development programme never gets started in the first place, or it slows down, loses its impetus and never reaches its goals. The commonest road-blocks include:

1. insufficiently compelling motivation in terms of beneficial outcomes;

2. lack of commitment from the chairman or other key gatekeepers;

3. insufficient budget allocated to the programme because of other priorities;

4. time pressures on the board;

5. unproductive competition between the directors;

6. rewards not linked to achievement of development objectives.

You need to answer each of these blocks by:

1. persuading the board of the benefits;

2. gaining commitment from other strong champions;

3. demonstrating the importance of having a board that is competent to lead the company into a profitable future;

4. accepting time pressures on directors, but showing that it's a matter of whether the board priority should be short-term tactics or the long-term health of the company;

5. highlighting the directors' duty to work together for the good of the company;

6. establishing a link between reward and development objectives.

Ultimately the chairman is responsible for most of these issues.

Action list:

1. Set and achieve objectives for continuous improvement in the quality and effectiveness of board performance including performance in a crisis.

2. Review regularly the degree to which the board's objectives are achieved.

3. Review regularly the quality of the board's decisions, advice and information received and consequent action taken.

4. Consider the impact on board effectiveness of directors' attitudes to handling risks, failure, ethical issues, change, commitment and challenges to their interpersonal relationships and their decision-making styles.

5. Identify and influence the strengths and weaknesses of individual directors where these affect the performance of the board as a whole.

6. Take appropriate action including the use of training and external specialists to maximize directors' efficiency and the effectiveness of board work.

SUMMARY

The effectiveness of a board is dependent upon:

■   board composition and organization;

■   clarity of the powers, roles and responsibilities of the board;

■   the management of the board meeting.

In this chapter you have seen four action lists that you should now be able to convert to checklists to assess the effectiveness of your own board and to indicate areas for development.

6

Director development

'In a recent survey 32% of organisations had a formal process of development for individual directors and 12% of organisations had a process of development for the board as a whole' (IoD, 1998b). You may be aware of a definition of director development as: 'The systematic maintenance, improvement and broadening of knowledge, experience and skills and the development of personal qualities helpful in the execution of the role as a director' (IoD, 1999). The process of director development should be owned and managed by the individual director. Of course, others such as development experts can offer extensive assistance in identifying needs and solutions in the areas of knowledge, experience, skills and personal qualities.

PRECONDITIONS FOR DIRECTOR DEVELOPMENT

Bob Garratt suggests that the following preconditions really make an added value investment in developing directorial competence:

▪ *Payment of director's fees to all executive and non-executive directors will concentrate their minds wonderfully on the direction-giving aspects of their work.*

▌ *Time and money budgets are needed for board, and individual director, development to give them both 'omniscience' and multi-disciplinary competence as they have usually been single-functional specialists.*

▌ *The chairman needs to accept, as is the law, that they are the 'boss of the board' and that it is their duty to ensure the development of board competence. This comes as a shock to most chairmen who often think that board development is a CEO role. It is not.*

▌ *There must be an induction, inclusion and competence-building process for each board member so that their roles, tasks and liabilities are codified and then their directorial attitudes, behaviours and knowledge are tested regularly.*

▌ *Investment in the directorial competence building process has to include some simple behavioural changes to let others in the organisation see that this person has directorial responsibilities and authority.*

Agreement is made that board development means an investment of a minimum of six days a year, plus individual director coaching.

(Garratt, 2000a)

Garratt suggests that the following six elements are needed for a board to identify its specific needs and plan a comprehensive development process:

1. *The 'Wake Up Call' (or reading the Riot Act) workshop – laying out the presently demanded board and director roles, tasks, liabilities and values, and mapping the growing volume of likely future ones.*
   If this does not wake up sufficient members of the board, then it is time to sell the company's shares – they are unlikely to survive even in the medium term.

2. *'Developing Strategic Thinking' workshop – dropping at least some of the directors' managerial and specialist roles so that they can learn how to take a more strategic stance – 'developing the Helicopter View'.*

3. *'Policy Formulation and Foresight' – two dimensions are:*

— 'softer' areas of purpose, vision, values and culture of the organisation – especially in relation to the creation of energy in the corporation to support the directors' key task of driving the enterprise forward whilst keeping it under prudent control. This is an often overlooked board role and usually pays handsome returns.

— 'harder' edge of monitoring the external environment, the daily newspaper reading rather than expensive on-line data gathering, knowing through constant tracking how your customers and competitors are moving. This then leads at least once a quarter into the Strategic Thinking day.

4. 'Effective Board Working' workshop – looking at the power ownership and control issues in the board and the organisation, and addressing and adapting any previous negative attitudes and behaviours with regard to the task (rational) elements and social process (emotional) elements of work.

5. 'Prudent Control' workshop – looking at the directorial control mechanisms and agreeing the ratios, trend lines and other benchmarks by which the board can understand the organisation.

6. 'Accountabilities' workshop – looking at the legal accountabilities of the board. As increased numbers of directors are fined or jailed for breaking the environmental pollution, or health and safety at work laws, this is an increasingly important area for collective agreement.

With the rapid acceptance by companies of 'triple bottom line' annual reporting of the financial, physical environmental, and societal bottom lines – all with independent audits against tough agreed measures – this is also becoming an item of great developmental interest for boards.

(Garratt, 2000a)

THE DIRECTOR DEVELOPMENT PROCESS

As a new director you go through a series of stages. You need to address and work upon each stage until it is in reasonable balance before you can go on to the next stage. You cannot leapfrog over them, as they are sequential and cumulative. You achieve your learning over time.

The stages of the process you, and all other newly appointed directors, will experience are:

1. *Induction.* It is important that this is handled well. It concerns introduction to the job of director and to the people with whom you will now be working. There should be a review of what is expected of you in your new role. The board may have to develop new working processes every time its membership changes, and it is not enough simply to include the new director into old ways of working. Common methods of induction include:

    – briefing papers;

    – internal visits;

    – introductions.

2. *Inclusion.* This requires energy from the rest of the board as it concerns building up rapport, trust and credibility so that you are accepted by and can work with fellow directors.

3. *Competence.* This is established by gaining technical capability and building social relationships.

4. *Development.* This is a continuous, almost lifelong process as directors are assigned fresh tasks and particular roles to fulfil to enable the company to cope strategically with changes in the market and environment.

5. *Effectiveness.* You will have reached this stage when competence is evidenced in all areas of your directorial activity.

6. *Transition.* You will have reached this stage when you move into a new role on the board, for example an executive director becoming non-executive or promoted to chief executive.

All organizations should specify the performance levels expected from their directors and should have a detailed framework for all the stages of the development. Figure 6.1 shows director development stages.

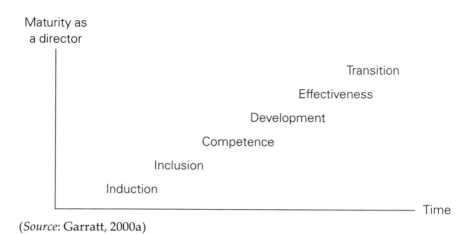

(*Source*: Garratt, 2000a)

Figure 6.1 *Director development stages*

Again, the results of IoD surveys of director preparation are not encouraging:

In a recent survey directors were asked how they prepared themselves or how they were prepared for their role as a company director.

No preparation	*35%*
Previous experience	*42%*
Professional/management qualification	*30%*
Career development	*30%*
Appropriate training courses	*27%*
Proper board inductions	*6%*

They were also asked how they thought individuals should be prepared for the role as a company director.

Proper board induction	*61%*
Specific courses	*59%*
Proven executive success	*47%*
Co-option to the board	*23%*

(Source: IoD, 1998b)

Here is an outline example of a formalized and structured development process for directors.

The development process for Business Link board members

At recruitment

▮ Explanation of the function of the organisation

▮ Outline list of services provided

At appointment

▮ Initial discussion and welcome (Chairman and Chief Executive)

▮ One to one with Chairman

▮ Explanation of director's role

▮ Explanation of business plan

▮ Explanation of partnership agenda, including briefing on individual partners

▮ Handover of written materials

▮ Introduction to senior staff

▮ Introduction to operational staff

At first board meeting

▮ Welcome and introduction to board members

▮ Support and attention through meeting

▮ Personal de-briefing after meeting

Over the longer term

▮ Member to spend time with a Personal Development Adviser

▮ After 3 or 4 months further meeting to identify outstanding concerns

Continuing development

▮ Occasional events designed to update members on the wider issues and developments affecting Business Links

▌ From time to time use an agenda item to develop through briefing and discussion understanding of wider developments.

(A development guide for Business Link board members, 1998)

DEVELOPMENT, TRAINING AND EDUCATION

Development is a complex process of professional and personal growth, of acquiring and increasing knowledge, experience and skills, and of enabling personal qualities to mature. The development process may involve activities that you might regard as training or education. They may be tactically appropriate as: 1) training assumes that there is a body of knowledge that the trainer possesses and can transfer to the trainee(s), ie the director or the board; and 2) education assumes that there are ideas and processes that can be transferred to the learner(s).

A survey reported by Revans (1984) focused upon the differences between training and development. A large majority (84 per cent) agreed that it is helpful to make the distinction. Their responses to particular statements gave the results shown in Table 6.1.

Training and education for directors

There are a variety of ways you can learn how to do something better. You can learn from your own experience. You can learn from your contractors, suppliers, partners, and customers. And you can learn from companies totally outside your business. All are crucial no matter where the knowledge comes from. The key to reaping a big return is to leverage that knowledge by replicating it throughout the company so that each unit is not learning in isolation and re-inventing the wheel again and again.

(Browne, CEO at BP, quoted in Prokesch, 1997)

A wide variety of training courses specifically designed for directors is provided by various training providers.

Table 6.1 *Differences between training and development*

	% Agreeing
Compared with Training	
Development involves self-motivation and people thinking for themselves.	73%
Development is more holistic and takes the whole situation into account.	70%
Development deals more with the long term.	63%
Development deals with no-right-answer situations.	57%
Compared with Development	
Training is specific and related to clearly identified needs.	70%
Training produces an extension of existing abilities.	39%
Training is done for you and to you.	28%

Research on training providers

According to a recent survey, training for existing and potential board members was provided by external providers in 56 per cent of organizations and internally provided by 10 per cent of organizations. The relevancy of the service provided by the external provider was as follows (IoD, 1998b):

IoD	83%
Other professional associations	64%
Specialist consultants	49%
Postgraduate business schools	41%
Management consultants	33%
Government agencies	28%
Individual agencies	22%

The preferred development method was as follows:

Short courses	58%
Coaching	34%
Board facilitation	26%
Programmes of learning	23%

The level of sophistication preferred in open courses for directors was as follows:

General fundamental, covering essential issues	57%
High level	28%
Intensive, exploring complex issues at length/in depth	27%

The Institute of Directors is an important provider of director development programmes. You will find details at Appendix 2.

Working with other people

You may develop fastest by working with other people. Many senior executives learn from a peer group, either inside or outside the company, or from an external network of people working in the same industry. Some find that discussing problems outside the industry is easier, especially when they recognize that what's keeping them awake at night is something shared by many other companies.

It helps to involve someone in your development processes so that he or she can:

▪ question your assumptions or the reality you are working in;

▪ reflect your ideas back to you;

▪ help you maintain the discipline of the process.

It is obviously important that your personal developer has the right combination of knowledge and personality to be a confident and supportive yet challenging helper.

Sources of ideas

A survey by Roffey Park in 1999 (Syrett and Lammiman, 1999) involving 120 chief executives, main board directors and senior managers identified the main sources of ideas as:

- discussion with a friend or colleague in this country;

- conference speaker;

- discussion with a friend or colleague in another country;

- private research;

- non-executive directorship;

- business school tutor;

- personal activity during a business trip abroad.

Personal feedback

Personal feedback is a process of managing information about people that you can use to aid your development process. The feedback might be direct from your boss and other colleagues, or it could be indirect in feedback questionnaires, such as 360-degree feedback taken from a wide range of your contacts. Feedback on your performance can let you know exactly where to aim your effort for the next period. It should provide information on the following:

- performance contribution as an individual and as a team or board member;

- business strategy, direction and performance;

- management style, leadership skills and decision making;

- communication.

This enables you to build on your strengths and develop in other areas required by the business. Development should be based around personal attributes, making use of the skills and expertise you have in your board. You can also improve your own!

In order to engage in your own development process it is most effective if you discuss or work with another person. This can be a fellow director, an outside consultant or a specialist member of the HR department. Ideally the other person should have a track record in this area and you should feel able to trust him or her with confidential information.

Once you know and own what you need to do, how do you develop effectively? To arrive at the right answer for you, you need help from the people in your organization who are paid to advise on this subject. These may be:

- a director responsible for director development – probably the chairman;

- your human resources staff;

- a coach;

- a mentor.

Coaching

Executive coaching is fast increasing as an effective means of development. What is essential is to find a coach with whom you can build rapport and who will facilitate your development, without imposing direction. That is driven by you. Clutterbuck (1998) identifies the following characteristics to be associated with coaching. The activity:

- is concerned with the task;

- focuses on skills and performance;

- agenda is set by the coach;

- feedback to the learner occurs through discussion;

- typically addresses a short-term development need.

Help is available in locating the best coach for you, once you know what you need to learn (see Appendix 7).

Mentoring

Some directors enjoy learning from mentors, or from becoming mentors themselves. Again this can be within the company, the industry or just a respected role model somewhere in your sphere of contacts.

Research has found that many organizations experienced problems with their mentoring schemes because it was assumed that all directors would be able to mentor. Most directors said that they benefited from being given a process to follow. Green and McBain (1995) and Green (1997) found that managers who received external mentoring had:

▪ increased understanding of barriers to personal performance and ways to overcome them (85 per cent);

▪ improved their understanding of the organization's vision, mission and objectives (85 per cent);

▪ greater clarity of personal vision (82 per cent);

▪ identified barriers to organizational performance and overcome them;

▪ improved performance against stated criteria (75 per cent);

▪ improved their ability to handle stress (73 per cent).

(from *Organisations and People*, August 1999, **6** (3))

Harsco

Harsco is a provider of on-site technology and services to steel mills. It has $1.7 billion turnover and operates in over 300 locations in over 30 countries with nearly 15,000 employees. The board has created a culture in which directors work closely with the senior managers of the operating divisions. Each division has at least one board member as mentor and larger divisions have two or three. The mentor relationship starts with the mentor visiting the division and meeting with senior management and as many levels of employees as possible. 'He listens, gives advice if there's advice to offer and he gets familiar with the operations.' The mentors can identify that the board's strategies are understood and being carried out.

'There's a great amount of trust and understanding required and it goes both ways. Directors and managers get to know each other better and develop a healthy respect for each other's background, specialisms, experience and workplace challenges.'

'Senior managers have come to appreciate directors as individuals who know and care about Harsco and its prospects not as aloof outsiders, detached and uninformed about the company's daily concerns.'

The mentoring programme is now in its fourth year and the first rotation of mentors is being planned.

(Source: Hathaway, 2000)

Being mentored

A mentor should respond to the needs of the mentee. This may involve being a:

▌ role model;

▌ sounding board;

▌ critical friend.

The mentor needs to recognize where the boundary of the relationship ceases and a different type of relationship exists. For example, a mentor may use some form of coaching style behaviours but the mentor would not set out development goals for the mentee nor would the mentor give direct feedback about how the mentee has been performing at work.

The life cycle of a mentoring relationship comprises the following stages:

▌ rapport building – developing trust;

▌ direction setting – setting goals for the relationship although the goals usually evolve;

▌ progress making – when experimentation and learning occur;

▌ maturation – where the relationship becomes mutual in terms of learning and support, and the mentee becomes more self-reliant;

▌ close down – where the formal relationship ends.

Being a mentor

When mentoring senior managers, directors start to hear about familiar problems from a different perspective. This presents the opportunity to:

▌ gain a lot of useful information about the issues and problems within the company;

▌ learn new ways of listening and talking;

▌ be role models for preferred organizational behaviour.

The outcomes are that trust is increased and the managers increase their confidence.

360-degree feedback

The system gathers comments about the individuals being assessed, about their task performance and the appropriateness of their behaviour in relation to organizational values from:

▌ their direct reports;

▌ their peers;

▌ their boss.

In some cases even the customers and suppliers become part of the process. It is a very rich source of information and creates good understanding of the issues but it takes a long time to process the resulting data and turn it into information. If directors budget time effectively, this should not cause difficulties. If they do not, 360-degree feedback can quickly get a bad name as an overly bureaucratic system.

Before implementing 360-degree feedback, the board should consider the following questions:

▌ Is the 360-degree process linked to the organizational strategy? (See Chapter 4.)

▌ Are the competency definitions and behavioural indicators clearly in line with the performance to be measured?

▌ Are there likely to be significant differences between the results that indicate strong and weak performers?

▌ Has the system been fully discussed by the board?

▌ Does the system have full board support?

Networks

You might find it helpful to make a map of the networks you currently use. The usual maps for networks are those where a person can get: 1) information of various kinds to help solve problems; and 2) help to get things done.

The resources mapped would normally be people with whom you have built up relationships, perhaps over many years. The most obvious candidates are your immediate colleagues, but you will probably have an address book of people that you have previously worked with, met at professional conferences, dealt with in other (even competitor) organizations, studied with or met socially. You can use these as a basis and improve the network by treating it conscientiously as a database to be developed, cleansed and managed.

This book is the result of a network that has been working over a period of five years. Within AMED it is very easy to form a network – you just advertise!

A survey by Roffey Park in 1999 involving 120 chief executives, main board directors and senior managers identified the main forms of networking opportunities as:

- industry network;

- professional network;

- dining club;

- boardroom forum;

- business school course;

- benchmarking group;

- local network.

Help is available in locating the right network for you, once you know what you wish to get out of the network (see Appendix 7).

Developing strategic thinking skills

'It's crucial to have thinking time. Key people in a business should spend at least 4–5 hours a week thinking of what needs to be done, how the team is functioning, what they've done well, what can be improved and which areas of the business need attention' (Bloch, head of executive coaching at Hay Management Consultants, 2000).

The director has to be prepared to ask questions:

- bringing frameworks into question;

- challenging existing ways of doing things;

- stepping outside the box and looking at the world position.

Using role models

You can easily underestimate the importance of peers and subordinates in organizations using role models as exemplars of good behaviour and practice:

> *I have recently begun to ask participants at corporate conferences to write down the names of people in their company who are consistently enthusiastic, welcoming and eager for new experiences. The question is always embarrassing. Last week when I put it to the top 200 managers from a global corporation they really struggled. After some hesitation they agreed to share this information. Only two of those present had reputations for being predictably positive, enthusiastic and optimistic. Even more worrying was the fact that not one member of the top team of seven was named.*

(Hunt, 2000)

Psychometric testing

Psychometrics can help you to gain self-understanding as a director. However, you need to treat these types of test with caution even if they are well validated. Most psychometric tests are self-completion and therefore only reveal what the respondents already believe about themselves. Also, you will find that scores on most tests change with changing life style or work style.

A widely used example of a validated psychometric test is the occupational personality questionnaire (OPQ). This questionnaire is designed to measure 30 separate aspects of an individual's behaviour, interests and personality characteristics in a work context. OPQ characteristics include: persuasive, controlling, independent, outgoing, affiliative, confident, modest, democratic, caring, practical, data rational, artistic, behavioural, traditional, change-oriented, conceptual, innovative, forward planning, detail-conscious, conscientious, relaxed, worrying, tough-minded, emotionally controlled, optimistic, critical, active, competitive, achieving and decisive. OPQ team roles include: co-ordinator, shaper, plant, monitor evaluator, resource investigator, completer, teamworker and implementer. Some organizations employ a number of psychometric tests. Confidence in the less than perfect evaluation methods can be increased if the results correlate.

Computer-based training

Your development may be aided by computer-based training. It is now readily available if you have the computer facilities. The main advantages are that you can carry the activities out at a time and place that suit you. However, as with every other training delivery method, it has supporters and critics.

Supporters argue that a well-designed learning package is highly cost-effective, especially with mechanistic areas of knowledge. Critics counter that few packages are well designed, even fewer deal with soft skill areas and almost none take any account of learning styles.

Non-executive directorships

You may be attracted to the idea of operating as a non-executive director on the board of a company outside the area of your current role or industry. While you will undoubtedly learn from the experience, this shouldn't be your sole motive, as you will be expected to contribute specific expertise to the board. You should also remember that you will have the same legal and financial responsibilities as the executive directors.

Contributing articles and speeches

Raising your own profile while publicizing the board's development programme in the media or at conferences can be a great development experience. If you write articles for the business media or present papers at conferences, you learn quickly through having to research and consider your material. You certainly get feedback, either through the letters page or delegates' comments or questions at the end.

A final suggestion for an effective development programme is that there is some form of regular follow-up. A central database should keep tabs on all individual directors' and the whole board's learning action plans, so that each director has regular and relevant contact from whoever is responsible for individual director development and board improvement. Only then will learning be truly effective and continuous. The ownership, however, remains with you.

Your favourite development process may be to explore relevant topics by reading texts written by business leaders or academics, reading newspapers or surfing the Internet. There is a list of useful readings in the References and Further reading sections at the back of the book.

SUMMARY

Unless directors set aside time for development then they will fail. If they devote all of their time to 'hands on' management and for their functional role then development will not happen.

The majority of organizations have no formal process of development for directors. The process of director development should be owned and managed by the individual director. Development processes can take many different forms. All of the methods are possible. To start the process, all you have to do is ask, to be curious. You'll be amazed by the positive response and help you get because learning is infectious.

7

The role of the developer

As we have said in previous chapters, you can get a great deal of assistance with director and board development processes if you employ development experts. The type of expert you use and the role that they play will depend upon the particular development needs of your organization, your board and the individual directors. In this chapter we examine the various roles that development experts can play in the process.

DEVELOPER ROLES

You could categorize types of developer as:

▌ development consultant;

▌ mentor;

▌ tutor;

▌ coach;

▌ guru;

▌ counsellor.

In Table 7.1 you can see how the different roles work. These roles are by no means fixed. There are times when the boundaries between roles will blur. Also many practitioners often define their roles in general rather than specific terms.

Another way of looking at the relationship between developer and client is to ask: who exercises design control over the solution to the director's or board's development needs? The different kinds of relationship are shown in Table 7.2:

1. In the minimal development relationship, the director or board knows what the problem is, is exercising design control over how to solve the problem and does not need the developer for knowledge but may require assistance with the process.

2. In the expert relationship, both parties know how to exercise design control but the developer can do a better job than the director. If not, it will collapse back into a contractor or outworker relationship.

3. In the guru relationship, the director does not know what the problem is and the consultant does. The big accounting and consulting firms tend to work this way, relying upon the dependent nature of board relationships to secure business and using existing and established business models and frameworks.

4. The development consultant relationship is one where the nature of the problem creates an explicit learning process in which both parties have to work together to develop effective ways of defining the problem before it can be solved. The development consultant brings expertise in problem defining and solving processes.

Starting the development process

When you begin a development process as a director, you normally start off from a position of being in your own reality (inside) and perceive the developer as external (outside). Table 7.3 illustrates the imposition of reality in the different kinds of relationship.

Table 7.1 *The different roles of developers*

	Development Consultant	Mentor	Tutor	Coach	Guru	Counsellor
Content	supplied by board or directors	knowledge and skills	knowledge and information	knowledge, skills and information	wisdom	self-awareness
Focus	supporting the working processes	capability and potential	provides insights and understanding	provides guidance, support and advice	provides insights and understanding	provides insights and self-understanding
Agenda	set by the chairman	mainly set by mentee	mainly set by tutor	mainly set by coach	set by guru	mainly set by learner
Direction of Learning	two-way	two-way	mainly tutor to student through a structured programme of learning	coach to learner	one-way: guru to pupil	mostly one-way: learner to counsellor. The counsellor is a good listener
Recipient Behaviour	working relationship	sees mentor as a role model; seeks approval	seeks advice	wants personal and professional goals to be set: positive attitude to new ideas and feedback	compliant	seeks frequent reassurance: can become dependent
Power of Developer	equal	low	high	medium	very high	low
Intensity of Relationship	medium	medium to high	medium	medium	low	low
Timescale	dependent on client	medium- to long-term	short-medium	often short-term	often in short bursts	often long-term

Table 7.2 *Design control*

		Director or Board	
		Knows	*Does not know*
Developer	*Knows*	2. Expert	3. Guru
	Does not know	1. Minimal development	4. Development consultant

(adapted from Faulkner and Boxer, 1995)

Table 7.3 *Imposition of reality*

		Director or Board	
		Knows	*Does not know*
Developer	*Knows*	Expert's knowledge is transferred to the client.	The guru's reality is superimposed on to the client's.
	Does not know	The developer may be used for assistance in the development process.	The development consultant accepts the client's frame of reference and then enables the client to recognize it and subsequently question it.

The beginning of development is characterized by:

- you, the recipient, being committed to development and prepared to engage actively in defining your questions and ways of working and accepting the power the consultant has in concentrating the process;

- both participants agreeing rules of engagement;

▪ the roles of the participants being agreed if the developer is working within the client's frame of reference.

When starting the development process, neither the developer nor recipient knows 'the answer' or even the best way of getting to the solution. The level of trust between the developer and recipient is abused if the developer gives advice as a guru or introduces a tried method.

Both the developer and the recipient need to work on what they perceive and what is hidden. Otherwise they may both fail to see how the director works as an individual and as a board member, what networks they have access to and how they use them.

The developer's role is to manage the process. This must include:

▪ asking questions;

▪ suggesting areas of research;

▪ bringing inconsistencies into play;

▪ noting conflicts between what is said and what is done.

Trust

In all forms of development, the developer has to establish trust. There are three types of trust:

1. calculative trust – the director calculates that the developer can help him or her and trusts the developer;

2. predictive trust – the director comes to believe that the developer will behave as the developer says he or she will;

3. friendship trust – the partners get to like each other as people and trust takes on a more personal aspect.

Power

The nature of power, its type and its use are critical when you are trying to distinguish between types of development. Power is the process by which one of the individuals influences the behaviour of the other. Power must be circumscribed if the development is to realize its aims and the individuals are to feel unconstrained, but equally if it is not present in some form the partners will not feel comfortable. Power and control can be separated into three dimensions:

1. extent – this measures the degree to which the parties can exercise control;

2. focus – defines the functional areas over which a party chooses to exercise control;

3. mechanism – the means by which control is exercised.

There will always be a tension between a party's desire to control and his or her willingness to trust. If a party exerts too much control this can threaten the quality of the relationship. A balance needs to be struck between the need to control and the need for a harmonious relationship.

Performance is often better when the consultant is less dominant so that the client is able to contribute fully. This helps the client cope with unfamiliar circumstances. As a director seeking development, you are usually the client so you need to be very sensitive to the power issues outlined here when making your choice of developer.

SUMMARY

Development experts can provide a great deal of assistance with director and board development processes. Key issues of trust and power are associated with the type of relationship formed with the developer, that is, whether the developer is a development consultant, mentor, tutor, coach, guru or counsellor.

8

The public and not-for-profit sectors

You will have seen from the preface to this book that there are a substantial number of people occupying director-type roles in organizations in the public and not-for-profit sectors. As you will see in this chapter, their duties are very similar.

The public and not-for-profit sectors are extremely large in the UK and comprise:

▌ The public sector:

- health authorities, local authorities and central government.

▌ The not-for-profit sector:

- Quasi-autonomous non-governmental organizations (quangos) are organizations whose board members are appointed by the government to perform a public function. There are about 5,500 quangos on whose boards sit around 100,000 appointed members.

- Non-governmental organizations (NGOs) include voluntary and charitable organizations. This term is often used in the international aid field.

- Charities are organizations that meet the strict conditions required for charity registration.

– Voluntary organizations have social or political aims but have not registered as charities or do not meet the criteria.

– Independent not-for-profit universities and hospitals, trade unions, professional associations and other similar organizations may make profits but do not distribute them.

You can see from Table 8.1 that the boundaries between the private, public and not-for-profit sectors are fuzzy.

Table 8.2 indicates the scale of public sector and not-for-profit organizations.

Table 8.1 *Boundaries between the private, public and not-for-profit sectors*

	'Pure' Organizations	*Hybrid Organizations with the Private Sector*	*Hybrid Organizations with the Public Sector*	*Hybrid Organizations with the Not-for-profit Sector*
Private Sector	companies	N/A	public sector organizations that are being privatized	co-operatives, mutual organizations, provident associations, independent schools
Public Sector	central government, local government, health authorities	public sector organizations that are being privatized	N/A	quangos, grant maintained schools, housing associations
Not-for-profit Sector	charities, voluntary organizations, campaigning organizations, trade unions, professional organizations	co-operatives, mutual organizations, provident associations, independent schools	quangos, grant maintained schools, housing associations	N/A

Table 8.2 *The scale of the public sector and not-for-profit organizations*

Type of Organization	Number of Boards	Number of Board Members or Equivalent
Charities	188,000 (1)	674,279 (2)
Schools	30,851 (1)	300,000 (3)
Local public spending bodies – including city technology colleges, further and higher education corporations, NHS trusts and health authorities	4,534 (4)	65,000–73,000(4)
Housing associations	2,200 (5)	N/A
Grant maintained schools	680 (1)	N/A
Advisory non-departmental public bodies – these include some royal commissions	563 (4)	6,780 (4)
Trade unions	219 (5)	N/A
Tribunal non-departmental public bodies – these operate within a field of law	69 (4)	19,882 (4)
Executive non-departmental public bodies (NDPB) – such as nationalized industries, public corporations and entities such as the Environment Agency	304 (4)	2,742 (4)
Board of visitors to penal establishments	137 (4)	1,823 (4)

Sources:

(1) *Britain 2000* (1999) HMSO
(2) Charity Commission, 2000
(3) DfEE Web site, September 2000
(4) Select Committee on Public Administration (1999) Quangos, sixth report, session 1998–99, vol 1, 9 November, House of Commons, London
(5) *Annual Abstract of Statistics 2000* (2000) HMSO

SIMILARITIES BETWEEN THE SECTORS

You may not have realized that the majority of corporate governance principles are the same for private, public and not-for-profit organizations. The key purpose, defined by the board of directors or governing body, is likely to be similar.

Organizations in the NHS provide a good example. The Institute of Directors have in recent years worked in collaboration with the NHS Executive, the National Association of Health Authorities and Trusts (NAHAT) and the NHS Trust Federation to adapt their board standards to fit the public and not-for-profit sectors. In 1996 the IoD published *Criteria for NHS Boards* and specified the key purpose of the board of an NHS trust as:

> *To ensure that the health authority or trust meets health and health care needs within the framework of overall government policy and priorities, and so plays its part in the wider NHS. The board does this by collectively directing the organization's affairs and accounting to Ministers and Parliament, through the NHS Executive and, for the way the legitimate needs of patients, the local community and other interested parties are met within the resources available.*

> *(IoD, 1996: 7)*

This definition is not very different from the key purpose of a company board, which focuses also on collective direction: 'The key purpose of the board is to ensure the company's prosperity by collectively directing the company's affairs whilst meeting the appropriate interests of its shareholders and relevant stakeholders' (IoD, 1999).

The tasks of the board

Again it should come as no surprise that the governing body should define their key tasks no matter whether the organization is in the private, public or not-for-profit sector. In most cases these key tasks will be very similar.

Business Link boards

The Institute of Directors have recently worked in collaboration with the Department of Trade and Industry and the National Business Link Partners to adapt their board standards to fit Business Link boards. In 1998, the IoD published *Good Practice for Board Members: A development guide for Business Link board members* (1998a) and identified the key task of a Business Link board as: 'to ensure that the Business Link meets its obligations'. To achieve this, the members should concentrate their energies in the following key areas:

▪ agreeing purpose and philosophy;

▪ determining strategy;

▪ setting policy;

▪ endorsing business plans;

▪ monitoring the achievement of plans;

▪ ensuring financial integrity;

▪ probity and accountability for public funds.

You can see that these key tasks are very similar to those defined for a company board. They were:

▪ establishing the purpose, vision and values;

▪ setting strategy and structure;

▪ delegating to management;

▪ exercising accountability to shareholders and being responsible to relevant stakeholders.

The reserved powers of the board

It has been discussed earlier that many boards over the last decade have developed statements of reserved powers. These statements have always been more common in the public and not-for-profit sectors. An example of a statement for reserved powers for an NHS board is listed below.

A statement of reserved powers for an NHS board

The Code of Accountability (NHS Executive, 1994) requires each NHS board to adopt a schedule of decisions that are reserved to the board. Although it is for each health authority and trust board to decide upon the detail of the financial and other control mechanisms that must be in place to maintain full and effective control over the organization, approval of the following items should be reserved for boards:

▪ strategy, business plans and budgets;

▪ standing orders, which should include a scheme of delegation;

▪ standing financial instructions;

▪ the establishment, terms of reference and reporting arrangements for all subcommittees acting on behalf of the authority or board;

▪ significant items of capital expenditure or disposal of assets;

▪ personnel policies including arrangements for the appointment, removal and remuneration of key staff;

▪ financial and performance reporting arrangements;

▪ audit arrangements;

▪ investment policy;

▪ approval of the annual report and accounts.

Areas that might be usefully covered in the scheme of delegation include:

▪ issuing, receiving, opening tenders and post-tender negotiations;

▪ sealing and signing of documents;

▪ delegation of budgets and approval to spend funds;

▪ operation of all detailed financial matters including bank accounts and banking procedures;

- management of non-exchequer funds;

- arrangements for the management of land, buildings and other assets;

- management and control of stocks;

- management and control of computer systems and facilities;

- recording and monitoring of payments under the losses and compensation regulations;

- making ex *gratia* payments;

- health and safety arrangements;

- data protection arrangements;

- insurance arrangements.

Again this statement is not fundamentally different from those produced by company boards. You may wish to compare it with the example we gave in Chapter 1.

The differing roles within the governing body

The chairman

You will now see how similar the role of the chairman is in all the sectors. Here is an example of the responsibilities of an NHS chairman.

Role of an NHS chairman

The chairman is responsible for leading the board and ensuring that it successfully discharges its overall responsibility for the organization as a whole. It is the chairman's role to:

- provide leadership to the board;

- enable all board members to make a full contribution to the board's affairs, and ensure that the board acts as a team;

- ensure that key and appropriate issues are discussed by the board in a timely manner;

▌ ensure the board has adequate support and is provided efficiently with all necessary data on which to base informed decisions;

▌ lead non-executive board members through a formally appointed remuneration committee of the main board on the appointment, appraisal and remuneration of the chief executive and other executive board members;

▌ appoint non-executive board members to an audit committee of the main board;

▌ advise the secretary of state through the regional member of the policy board on the performance of non-executive board members.

(Source: NHS Executive, 1994)

These are very similar to the duties of a company chairman discussed in Chapter 2.

The responsibilities of a charity trustee

The Charities Acts of 1992 and 1993 govern charities. The Charity Commission (1995) states that all trustees have full responsibility for their charity and must:

▌ act together and in person and not delegate control of the charity to others;

▌ act strictly in accordance with the charity's affairs prudently and take a long-term as well as a short-term view;

▌ not derive any personal benefit or gain from the charity;

▌ take proper professional advice on matters in which they are not themselves competent.

DIFFERENCES BETWEEN THE SECTORS

There are, of course, differences and many are subtle. They include:

▌ different values and culture;

▌ multiple stakeholder base for accountability;

I numerous and vague objectives;

I difficulties in monitoring performance;

I management structures and governance.

We discuss these issues below.

Different values and culture

Public sector and not-for-profit organizations are often at their most effective when the people involved share common values and assumptions about the organization's purpose and its style of operation. In many cases the values and culture have been defined by their governing body. For example, the values of an NHS trust were defined by the NHS Executive (1994):

> *There are 3 crucial public service values that must underpin the work of the Health Service.*
>
> *Accountability – everything done by those who work in the NHS must be able to stand the test of parliamentary scrutiny, public judgements on propriety and professional codes of conduct.*
>
> *Probity – There should be an absolute standard of honesty in dealing with the assets of the NHS: integrity should be the hall mark of all personal conduct in decisions affecting patients, staff and suppliers and in the use of information acquired in the course of NHS duties.*
>
> *Openness – there should be sufficient transparency about NHS activities to promote confidence between the NHS authority or trust and its staff, patients and the public.*

Superficially, these values are not very different from the private sector ones discussed in Chapter 1. However, there are generally felt to be significant differences beneath the surface. These differences can be quite difficult to identify but are represented through symptoms such as informal dress, cramped offices and large numbers of endlessly long committee meetings. This evidence often hides the deep-seated differences in people's values and beliefs that are really at the root of the sector differences.

Many not-for-profit organizations have unpaid governing bodies whose members may not have management experience. In addition, they rely upon the voluntary commitment of people involved in the organization. With such a degree of voluntary commitment, people expect to have their views listened to and to be actively involved in decision making.

Many directors have found that 'insensitive trampling on cherished values quickly results in demotivation and lengthy argument' (Hudson, 1995: 37). If you're a director or chairman of such an organization, you may already have experienced the problem of getting director colleagues to give up even more of their unpaid time to attend so-called training sessions. You will recognize the need to persuade colleagues of the investment value of planning and participating in well-organized development activities.

Multiplicity of stakeholders for accountability

In the private sector, there is usually a relatively straightforward relationship between the company and the customer. The company supplies customers with goods and services, and the directors are accountable to shareholders for the stewardship of the business. In the public sector, the public authorities supply public services and are accountable to the voters. In the not-for-profit organization, donors provide money, which the organizations use to provide services. Board members may be accountable to the donors and fund-raisers but there is often a weak link between these stakeholders and the service users.

Let's consider some examples.

Accountability in the school sector

Within the school sector there is a tradition of political and local accountability. The 1988 Education Reform Act and subsequent legislation have increased the power of central government in curriculum matters, inspection and funding arrangements. School governing bodies have been given greater responsibilities over expenditure, plans and health and safety. There is a statutory requirement for publicly maintained schools to have governing bodies. The Department for Education and Employment issues regulations that specify what these governing bodies can and cannot do.

Many governing bodies include keen parents but there is a general shortage of appointed experts. The headteacher is frequently perceived as the only person with knowledge of the substance and detail of national and local government education policies. The agendas are often prescribed by national and local government. Many schools are concerned with how to get the board to comprehend information and are constantly thinking of ways of presenting information as simply and clearly as possible.

Accountability in universities and colleges

Universities have for many years been independent while receiving financial support from the government. In the 80s and early 90s, all the polytechnics and many colleges of higher education were established as universities and placed in this sector. Funding is organized by the national Higher Education Funding Councils, which have set up quality assurance procedures for all higher education courses.

Central government legislation removed all FE colleges from local authority control in 1993 and established them as independent incorporated bodies whose governors took on responsibilities equivalent to those of company directors. All FE colleges are subject to rigorous Further Education Funding Council (FEFC) quality assessments every four years.

In contrast with the majority of schools, universities and colleges have been able to appoint to their boards members who bring substantial business and management experience.

Difficulties in monitoring performance

Many not-for-profit organizations (particularly those in the social, health, educational, environmental and spiritual fields) find great difficulty in determining clear, quantifiable and objective goals. They cannot simply use a financial bottom line of profit or a discounted cash flow technique to guide their choice of future priorities and investment. They usually have to rely on internal negotiation with multiple stakeholders to agree priorities between financial viability and the achievement of the organization's purpose and vision.

In this situation it becomes very difficult to measure and monitor their achievements. In addition, they may face greater levels of accountability. For example, the chief executives of all NHS bodies have a responsibility not only to their boards but also through the accounting officer to Parliament, ie there is a dual line of accountability.

Management structures and governance

Because many not-for-profit organizations have multiple stakeholders, they frequently develop complex management structures and processes to consult, co-ordinate and get things done. 'Even organisations that have streamlined their structures [in the not-for-profit sector] often have more intricate arrangements than their equivalent sized organisations in the private sector' (Hudson, 1995: 36).

There is often tension between professional management and enthusiastic volunteer activists. Directors may be chosen for their support for the CEO and for their contacts. Many members of not-for-profit sector governing boards have little governance expertise. Despite having definitions of their purpose and powers, they often perceive their role as:

■ overseeing the work and the finances of the organization – simply acting as a check on housekeeping efficiency and propriety;

■ rubber-stamping executive decisions;

■ being used by the CEO as a back stop to take decisions that might be difficult or controversial, for example the pay of a professional director;

■ forming a link with key stakeholders and sources of funding;

■ acting as a valuable source of information for the CEO.

Cornforth has found: 'there is little thought devoted to whether it [the board in not-for-profit organizations] performs its duties well or to whether governance is an opportunity to add value to the organisation's work' (Cornforth and Edwards, 1999). He has also shown that charity boards frequently get involved in management and operational activities and that few charity boards devote time to their own development.

Competencies of public and not-for-profit organization board members

Richard Chaitt (1993) has identified six competencies that are related to effective board performance:

1. *Contextual dimension.* The board understands and takes into account the values and beliefs of the organization it governs.

2. *Educational dimension.* The board ensures that board members are well informed about the organization and the board's role, responsibility and performance.

3. *Interpersonal dimensions.* The board nurtures the development of members as a group and fosters a sense of cohesion.

4. *Analytical dimension.* The board recognizes complexities in the issues it faces and draws upon different perspectives to find appropriate solutions.

5. *The political dimension.* The board accepts the need to develop healthy relationships with key constituencies.

6. *The strategic dimension.* The board helps ensure a strategic approach to the organization's future.

SUMMARY

The public and not-for-profit sectors in the UK are large and varied. The majority of corporate governance principles are the same for organizations in all the sectors – private, public and not-for-profit. The differences between the sectors involve differences in:

▌ values and culture;

▌ accountability processes;

▌ the nature of the organization's objectives;

▌ monitoring performance;

▌ management structure.

9

Case studies

On the following pages you will see accounts from real organizations of development activities they established to meet particular needs at particular stages in their own organizational development. We have reproduced these in the hope that you will be able to use in your own organization some of the ideas you meet. We suggest you read all the cases, as many of the methods may work in different types of organizations. The cases are:

1. Securicor – developing directors on main boards and subsidiaries;

2. Anglian Water plc – director development;

3. Dearle and Henderson – developing a professional partnership;

4. Flemings investment bank – a global development programme;

5. BDO Stoy Hayward – partner development;

6. Shandwick International – director development;

7. 3i – independent director programme;

8. A school governing body – governor development;

9. NHS South West board – director development;

10. Oxfam GB – council development;

11. Action learning – An action learning facilitator's viewpoint.

CASE 1 – SECURICOR

Key issues

This case discusses two phases of developing directors on main boards and subsidiaries. It starts with a sudden need to develop many managers appointed as directors of subsidiary companies. The need then changes to individually focused development.

Introduction

Securicor is an international business-to-business group specializing in security, distribution, communications and ancillary support services. It began in 1935 and now operates in over 30 countries around the world. It is market leader in many of its businesses.

Context for change

Roger Wiggs, the group chief executive, was promoted from Securicor's international division in 1988. A divisional structure was established that separated the main board and the centre from five group divisions. Each division comprised four or more independent subsidiary companies. By 1990, four divisions had been established: security, parcels, communications and business services. By 1997 the business services division was absorbed into the other three. Key components of the changes included:

▪ a number of existing managers appointed as directors;

▪ development of the corporate governance theme as a result of the Cadbury Report on corporate governance (1992);

▌ segmented reporting of business activities (P & L responsibility established at company level);

▌ significant improvement in IT utilization;

▌ directors expected to understand the whole of their business, rather than just their own function.

The director development programme (DDP)

In 1991, Peter Humphrey, the then group personnel director, established with the board the need to 'ground the new directors'. Peter Stansfield, the then group HR manager, researched and developed a director development programme. The IoD director programme was used as a base with other modules added and the whole programme 'Securicorized' and run in-house. It commenced as seven modules:

▌ legal duties and role of the company director;

▌ finance for directors;

▌ effective marketing strategies;

▌ strategic business direction;

▌ improving business performance (a quality module);

▌ the human dimension of business;

▌ organizing for tomorrow (an organization development module).

The modules counted towards the IoD diploma in company direction. An eighth module, budget and profit planning, was added after the programme began.

The programme was launched in April 1992, at a major conference attended by 200 directors and senior managers from Securicor's companies in Europe. The programme was owned and driven hard by the group chief executive. Costs were charged back to participant companies. In 1993, 90 directors completed the programme. Directors from main board, division executive and subsidiary companies were mixed on the various modules. By 1994, 70 directors from subsidiary companies, plus promotions and arrivals, had completed the programme.

Director development programme achievements

The programme was viewed as a 'sheep dip' approach to ground everyone in the basics as quickly and professionally as possible. It achieved this broad goal and is credited with speeding up the rate of change in the company culture. The programme was expensive to develop and to run, yet seen as good value. Most of those who attended wanted more and asked 'what now?' Measurement of results was limited to feedback questionnaires and observation. Specific achievements included:

▌ common language: for example, at meetings with strategy people there is now a shared foundation and understanding of their terms and focus;

▌ common starting-point of knowledge and understanding;

▌ demystification of much of the specialized language and knowledge;

▌ better discussion and involvement;

▌ improved challenging and decision making.

In addition to the programme, a number of directors also became non-executive directors of one of the other subsidiary companies. This helped them to understand the strengths and weaknesses of highly focused executive directors and the value of non-executive directors. It is also excellent practice for viewing a company from a board perspective.

Securicor is part of IMD, a consortium of 25 companies, including: Barclays, BT, Marks & Spencer, Metropolitan Police and Rolls-Royce. The IMD goal is for 'cost effective, international, future-focused learning environments for executive development'. Directors attend two-week courses, based on action learning, with feedback, exposure and benchmarking in Week 1, and a specific project in Week 2.

Individual director development

'We don't have a programme. We have a process' (Michael Alsop, divisional development manager). The sheep dip approach had met a particular and timely need. Ongoing director development needed to be both effective and personal. In general, there were seen to be too many solutions from too many suppliers to training needs that had not been clearly identified. Michael Alsop developed a programme/ process. It has been in use for two years in four companies in the UK and is being rolled out internationally.

The main feature is the starting-point – the director development needs analysis. There are six clear steps, which require several days of the director's time to confirm the needs, the best solutions and a development plan. Each director is guided by the development manager the first time. A strong element of the process is 360-degree feedback. Solutions include:

▌ business school programmes – these have grown from nil to be the main source;

▌ in-house mentoring;

▌ outreach – networking with opposite numbers in other companies;

▌ reading;

▌ interviews with other directors in the division or group;

▌ workshops and courses, for example for languages or public speaking.

The solutions are monitored by HR for apparent satisfaction and fit with Securicor values and language. But HR-approved solutions are not mandatory.

Individual achievements

The main individual achievements involve awareness and responsibility. Many directors have not previously had time or guidance to learn how to analyse a personal development need and apply a solution likely to be effective. Before the DDP, formal training had been no one's apparent responsibility. Now it is very clear that director development is the responsibility of the individual director. Anecdotal examples of achievements are specific directors who have developed confidence and skill in public speaking, finance, strategy, marketing and foreign languages.

Director development issues for the next few years

Issues include:

1. Transnational management.

2. Environmental scanning.

3. Consistency of approach.

4. Succession development.

5. Use of IT for competitive advantage and e-commerce.

6. Group permission and identity – each company does its own thing.

7. Can we offer people meaningful development from the group? Or are their development and career now focused on the company or division they work for? Where are the specialist technical areas now, and in what circumstances are they appropriate?

(Sources: interviews with Peter Humphrey, group personnel director, retired, on 12 August 1999; Peter Stansfield, HR director, on 9 December 1999, 10 February 2000 and 11 April 2000; and Mike Alsop, divisional development manager, on 9 December 1999.)

CASE 2 – ANGLIAN WATER PLC

Key issues

This case discusses two phases of director and management development. Phase 1 involves a broad approach to transform a company following privatization and focuses on team, organization and skills development. Phase 2 involves a new MD and executive directors using open assessments, living the espoused values and providing a role model for the organization.

Introduction

Anglian Water plc was privatized in 1989. The shareholders expected a rapid reduction in costs, primarily staff. Alan Smith, the chief executive, was determined that Anglian would avoid the mistakes of other privatized industries that lost quality and customer service in their haste to cut costs. In the 1990s many development programmes were initiated to change the board, management and culture from command and control to customer focus and bottom-up change. Since 1989, Anglian Water has:

▋ reduced its workforce by 20 per cent – over 1,000 people;

▋ reduced its management hierarchy from 11 levels to 5;

▋ made consistent profits and rated well in the FTSE 100;

▋ expanded non-regulated services overseas;

▋ attained a reputation as a benchmark utility worldwide in terms of performance for its wide range of stakeholders;

▋ established open communication that includes executive and non-executive directors in six-monthly unscripted sessions with all staff.

The group had a turnover of over £800 million in 1999 with a profit before tax and exceptionals of £258 million. Its current vision is to become the UK's leading water and waste water company by 2002, and one of the foremost in the world by 2007. The substantive changes in board, director and staff development took place in two major phases.

Phase 1: executive stretch and transformational journey

In 1993–95 a substantial reorganization reduced the layers of management from 11 to 5 and focused the workforce outwards on the creation of a customer-oriented business. This reduced white-collar jobs by 33 per cent and saved £40 million. It also exposed Anglian to the likelihood of joining the many failed re-engineering programmes that had ignored people needs. Anglian discovered and dealt with the fact that many staff were demoralized because they felt that they had no effective line manager.

Alan Smith, with the board's backing, sponsored an 'executive stretch' programme, designed and provided by Dr Ronnie Lessem of City University. The learning from and success of the programme with directors led the board to run an 'executive stretch for all' programme. This became known as the 'transformational journey'.

The programme / process has four inputs designed to deliver benefits (outputs):

1. relationships development: self-awareness and communications skills;

2. teamwork: ability to work within and contribute to the growth and development of the work team;

3. operational effectiveness: ability to improve short- to mid-term business/process performance;

4. sustainability: long-term business and environmental improvements.

The team learning cycle developed creativity and innovation that led to acting on new ideas. The model is from Nonaka and Takeuchi's knowledge creation cycle. The next stage had a company facilitator and involved sharing experiences and learning, and deciding on the way forward for the team. Over six months, each team enacted the self-managed learning exercise and explored the practical relevance of the workshop.

From 1995–97, 3,000 Anglian Water employees (over 300 teams) enrolled voluntarily on the 'journey'. The results were plotted using employee opinion surveys, facilitated self-assessment of team competencies and data from a two-day review and data collection event. The benefits were subjective and confirmed as:

▌ Self and team development.

▌ Organizational development: innovation, flexible working practices and operational efficiency.

▌ Skills development.

All teams reported an improvement in their learning competencies. It is significant that those reporting high scores on relationship abilities also performed better than average on other team skills.

In parallel with the journey, an ambition for Anglian to become a learning organization was realized in the form of the 'university of water'. Knowledge was to be Anglian's strategic business link and the university aimed to promote the exchange of knowledge between different parts of the organization. It set up best practice networks to provide better customer service, enhance commercial success and deliver quality products and services. This was based on the teaching of David Garvin and Nonaka. Anglian confirmed 11 basic principles of learning that included: 1) 'we ensure that learning and business success are linked'; and 2) 'we recognise that individuals learn in teams'. These initiatives have created the conditions for a learning organization with involvement in learning at all levels, and helped to assure the future for Anglian Water and its stakeholders.

Phase 2: in pursuit of world class

In 1997 Chris Mellor, the finance director, became group managing director. He reviewed and refocused the many initiatives being undertaken. He also recruited Clive Morton, author of *Beyond World Class*, as HR director. Initially Clive was heavily involved in changing relations with the unions from confrontational to partnership. He then focused on board and director development. The emphasis was on development of the vision and values, along with the behaviour to support them from top to bottom. Each director was put through open assessment, which involved:

▪ Myers-Briggs;

▪ action profiling – an external consultant coaching the director through analysis, feedback and learning;

▪ Belbin's team skills.

Each director knows the others' assessments. The value of using three less-than-perfect evaluation methods is that the overall picture correlates extremely well with people's perceptions of each individual. In engineering this is known as 'triangulation of error'. It is by doing more than one test, and getting perceptions of others that real value (and learning) is obtained.

Learning, exposure, sharing and working beyond the fear of exposure that most directors feel are key facets. 'Power to lead', a weekend course with directors from other companies, is also used and helps to flush out many of the emotional pressures.

Most, but not all, directors have considered this a watershed. The shared results mean that they know one another's 'hot buttons' and are aware of their own. They use their knowledge of one another to get greater involvement. Consultants and coaches are used for 'top up' sessions and to take them to the next stage of their learning. This is true throughout the company. A key quote of Chris Mellor's is: 'If we were a football team there would be no question of spending resources on coaching.'

All the executive directors have also been through the IoD director development programme. So far there has been no development of non-executives. Director evaluation and selection are similar to those for managers, with heavy emphasis on organizational fit. Anglian has also introduced the balanced business scorecard with the standard quadrants, plus measuring people development. The current emphasis is to focus on how to measure people development and to become very good at it.

Chris Mellor has underlined the focus on vision and values. This is issued to all management and staff along with a letter from him that clarifies his beliefs about leadership and how they link to the values. The board members are expected to live the vision and values. Every six months 'vision and value' sessions are held around the country for up to 500 management and staff at a time. A director attending the session is expected to relate what is happening across the company regarding vision and values, and take part in unscripted questions and answers.

(Sources: interviews with Clive Morton, 6 and 9 December 1999; Morton, (permission given to quote from his book).)

CASE 3 – DEARLE AND HENDERSON

Key issues

This case discusses the move of an organization from a partnership to a private limited company, with expansion by acquisition and organic growth, significant culture change and the development of the board and senior management.

Introduction

Dearle and Henderson was formed in 1908 as a professional surveyors practice. In 1992 the organization changed from a partnership of seven to a private limited company following a combination of unrelated events:

▊ a bid from an engineering company for majority ownership;

▊ negative customer feedback in a survey;

▊ change of regulatory environment;

▊ poor economic conditions;

▊ partners about to retire.

In 10 years, Dearle and Henderson has grown revenues by 400 per cent to £12 million, with staff increased from 80 to 200 through merger and organic growth. During this period the governing structure has evolved as the organization has grown from 10 partners to 26 directors.

The chairman and chief executive

Alan Yates, the remaining partner, took up the combined role on the condition that the director element was professionalized and a strategic review begun to carry out his mandate for change. The roles were combined because in a growing small and medium-sized enterprise, still operating as a partnership in style, he said, 'we need cohesion as opposed to democracy'. Aware of the importance of his own contribution, Alan Yates saw the need to be a role model within the organization in championing and managing change. He said he wanted 'to continually test assumptions, and test the way my business is looked at'. So, he has consistently looked outside the organization through:

▊ benchmarking;

▊ non-executive directorships;

▮ industry sector appointments;

▮ a visiting professorship;

▮ undertaking a master's programme.

As he needed to carry his colleagues with him, he employed inclusion techniques that have taken them to higher degrees of self-awareness. They have discussed the need to reduce interpersonal barriers to achieve faster decision making, and increase innovation to spur growth. However, feedback from directors has indicated that his colleagues are not sure if he is in a chairman or chief executive role.

The directors

Initially two types of director were created: 1) operational directors – in effect, partners without management responsibility; and 2) executive directors. The board had to shrug off the notion that the shareholder / proprietor was still part of the senior management team. The main challenge has been to get directors to play to their professional strengths and make the operational role as rewarding and relevant as the executive role. The external focus of the board has been emphasized: 'it's about advising clients on their strategic property interests, not debating the colour of our toilet paper'. Attitude surveys were used to measure the extent of the difficulties clients had experienced in dealing with the business. As a result of concerns identified in the surveys, task forces were set up to involve directors in the teams dealing with clients.

To assist in the culture change, director development was introduced initially as a free-for-all. But it was ineffective because training had traditionally been seen as a form of punishment or as deriving from the need to know about some new regulation or market change. Also, some directors didn't know how to use this new opportunity effectively, while others needed no encouragement. Structured director development was later introduced with:

▮ personal development plans;

▮ learning objectives;

▮ personal budgets for development purposes.

The board

Since 1992 the management structure has been kept under constant review in order to address customer needs and to ensure that the ongoing process of internal employment is maintained.

Within the current structure (Figure 9.1):

▌ A board of seven directors focused on strategy and policy. It included the two youngest directors to ensure effective links with the new thinking in the organization and to assist their own director development.

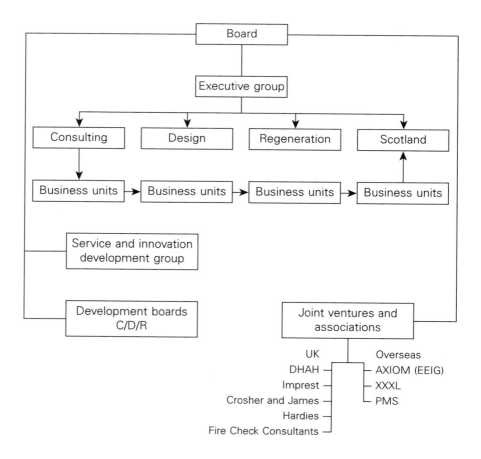

Figure 9.1 *Dearle and Henderson board and management structure*

▌ An executive group, including the heads of the support groups, to implement the strategy.

▌ The remaining operational directors are allocated to business units.

Board team development through regular away days was introduced. Alan Yates, the chairman, continues to be enthusiastic about inclusion techniques. For example, using principles taught on his master's programme, envisioning exercises were introduced to get the board to look to the future and shape the organization. Additionally, psychometric tools have been used 'to bring maps and lenses to the board' to see how they might work more effectively together. Alan Yates has also encouraged the board to find external mentors. He was reported as saying: 'You become so wound up in strategy that you forget you've got real talent around you'. If he had his time again, he says he would have built more time into his day 'to listen generously'. He is also a strong advocate of the need to constantly address the internal climate – on defining and actioning on the soft things like culture and values and internal communication – to support the change agenda.

Succession planning

As in other professional organizations, the challenge is to motivate the level below director to maintain learning and develop the next tranche of leaders. A start has been made by appointing young directors but there is a need to open up the career and management structure for talented people to continue to grow within the organization.

(Source: interview with Alan Yates, chairman and chief executive, on 21 October 1999 and endorsed through a further conversation, on 11 December 2000.)

CASE 4 – FLEMINGS INVESTMENT BANK

Key issues

This case examines the need to identify and develop key leaders through a global development programme within a company.

Introduction

Flemings (part of Chase Manhattan since its acquisition in 2000) was a family-owned investment bank with over 8,000 staff in 64 offices in 44 countries:

▌ In 1990 there was no central training function in place.

▌ In 1995 a central training function operating from London was established.

▌ In 1997 a global senior director development programme was launched.

This case study describes the global senior development programme.

Selection of participants

The participants selected for the programme were senior directors, deemed to be capable of at least two more career moves and identified as part of the succession planning process. They included all of the most senior directors but excluded the chief executive and the head of one of the major business divisions.

The programme

The programme was launched on two separate two-day sessions with 40 participants attending each one. The programme included a challenging input from Professor Gary Hamel – renowned management guru and visiting professor of strategy at London Business School.

The launch session initiated a 360-degree individual feedback process for each participant. All participants received feedback on the important factors for success in their specific job roles and their performance in these factors. Feedback came from

▌ their boss;

▌ their peers;

▌ their direct reports;

▌ themselves.

Following the launch and this feedback, each participant was encouraged to set up his or her own development plan. The organization believes this stage is a key factor in the success of any senior development programme, especially at director level since the ownership of the process belongs to the individual. In this way the process becomes a learning activity rather than training or development. 'I will be responsible for developing my skills. The organisation, in return, will give me feedback and the opportunity to learn and to practise what I've learnt' (an extract from a course participant on the banking and financial training programme).

The 360-degree benchmarking process also provided information on the factors most important for success at this senior level in Flemings. The four most important factors were:

1. leading employees;

2. hiring talented staff;

3. resourcefulness;

4. decisiveness.

In these areas the organization sought to concentrate on individual learning activities, including:

▌ individual coaching (internal and external);

▌ mentoring;

▌ distance learning;

▌ reading;

▌ structured job moves;

▌ external courses and seminars.

Senior executives were encouraged to take on non-executive directorships and seek secondments to enhance their skill. A central database was created to capture the learning actions of each director, and individual HR staff were tasked with regular monitoring meetings.

Key success factors

To succeed, a director development process needs:

- a high-profile launch;

- chief executive to take a full part;

- ownership by the individual directors of their own development;

- 360-degree feedback;

- 20 per cent of resources in the launch and 80 per cent in the follow-up;

- awareness of different styles of effective learning;

- process embedded in corporate culture and vision;

- link to performance and reward;

- follow-up with cross-company as well as individual development.

Outcomes

While the participants increased their learning, the major fault in this programme was that it was not embedded into the corporate culture of the organization. It was not linked to Flemings vision, values, appraisal system and succession planning processes. This meant that although individuals learnt, the learning was not linked directly to their performance or to their reward. It also meant that no formal training on common needs was developed or conducted across the company.

What next?

An external consultancy was engaged to help articulate the corporate vision and culture. Company-wide appraisal and succession planning processes have been introduced and clearer performance criteria introduced. The intention was to retain the emphasis on individual learning but now to embed that into the culture and people systems of the company.

(Source: Keith Griffiths, group training and development director, Flemings, 1990–2000.)

CASE 5 – BDO STOY HAYWARD

Key issues

This case examines one solution for partner development, which arose from the need for partners to remain fresh, motivated and on top of the underlying changes in the marketplace.

Introduction

BDO Stoy Hayward is a leading firm of chartered accountants and the UK member of BDO, the international accounting and consulting group. It has over 300 partners and 2,000 staff in the UK. In 1995 its current business strategy was developed – to specialize in providing expert advice to businesses that aspire to grow. Its client base ranges from business start-ups to multinational businesses that are mainly under entrepreneurial management.

Partner development

Being the owner-manager in a professional service firm is increasingly a way-of-life decision. Fee-earning activities, business development roles, and managing people and change are increasingly complex and demanding responsibilities. Burn-out is a real issue. So keeping fresh, motivated and on top of the underlying changes in the marketplace are essential if partners are to continue to add value to the client base.

The managing partner and the management executive took a view that to avoid these downsides, an educational sabbatical should be taken. The deal for partners was that they should take at least a month out to attend a reputable business school. It should ideally be outside the UK so that contact with clients and the firm was minimized. And they should learn, think and discuss. On their return they were expected to disseminate the learning to colleagues in the firm, but the methodology was not clarified.

The benefits of attending schools like Insead, Oxford and Harvard were felt in terms of receiving top-notch academic input on contemporary thinking, and mingling with colleagues typical of the firm's client base. The benefits of being re-energized were incalculable.

When the programme was launched, the partnership considered how this new intellectual capital could be enhanced. What emerged was a business education programme for the partnership. It was based on core areas of knowledge about which clients typically sought partners' views – strategy, leading change, managing growth, organizational dynamics and so on. With some facilitation from Ashridge on structure and content, a programme emerged that was taught by a team of partners initially to colleagues and then to all levels of staff.

A strong learning experience and a galvanizing of the firm's cultural identity were the benefits of a combination of:

▌ theory;

▌ case studies using either clients of the firm or organizations in the firm's target market;

▌ the firm's own research;

▌ group discussion.

Three main results arose. The process reinforced the partners' learning, as they had to deliver it. It strengthened the firm's business and people strategy by focusing on the issues of the target market. The learning was delivered by people who advised clients on a daily basis. This proved a very powerful combination and has resulted in further training sessions again delivered by partners. The approach has been warmly welcomed by partners and has demonstrated the commitment to training and education within the firm.

CASE 6 – SHANDWICK INTERNATIONAL

Key issues

The case examines how an international organization recognized the need to produce a coherent development programme for directors in companies around the world to think like businesspeople rather than public relations practitioners, unify strategy and take the business to its next stage of growth.

Introduction

Shandwick was founded in the UK in 1974 and was listed on the UK Stock Exchange in 1985. The business grew dynamically through acquisition, and the years 1994–98 were necessarily spent in consolidation. Company brand names were rationalized and like businesses were merged.

In early 1998, financial gearing issues and the attractive prospect of cross-selling opportunities prompted Shandwick plc, with 2,300 employees round the world, to seek a tie-up with an international communications group. First it decided to streamline the global operation. The operating companies were focused on two main brands, Shandwick International and Golin Harris, under a newly named holding company, International Public Relations plc. The eight UK companies were rationalized to reflect practice specialities. After talking to several suitors, International PR was bought by The Interpublic Group of Companies, Inc and the stock market listing moved to Nasdaq.

This case is concerned with Shandwick International. The Shandwick brand is now marketed by region, rather than as previously by each operating company. This change from autonomous operating companies also provided the first real opportunity for a centralized director and management development programme, run through the co-ordination of three hubs in Asia, Europe and the United States.

Vision

Shandwick's vision was to be the largest worldwide PR company. It aimed to achieve this through organic growth and acquisition with the intention of changing its culture to one of business consultancy.

Learning from the previous director development programme

In 1997 Shandwick had run a director development programme for its UK businesses. This consisted of four modules, which were piloted on the CEOs and finance directors:

1. strategic thinking;

2. finance;

3. people;

4. Shandwick products and practices.

This was refined and rolled out to some 60 directors in the UK. Learnings about the programme were:

▌ Strategic thinking needed to be less academic and more pragmatic, dealing with issues facing the UK boards.

▌ The Shandwick products and practices module was dropped, as the subject was already familiar to delegates.

▌ The people module was changed to reflect the issues with which directors felt they frequently needed help.

In general, the programme was considered to have been a success.

CEO development programme

Following the success of the director development programme, Shandwick created a programme for CEOs, with the emphasis on running a global business and working more closely together across the Shandwick companies around the world. This involved close liaison between those responsible for the programme in the three regional hubs, London, New York and Singapore. The programme will involve CEOs around the world, and includes the following modules:

1. psychometric testing followed by a post-results away day;

2. external context and global business dynamics;

3. global challenges that face Shandwick and planning how to move on.

At the end of the third module, CEOs will be set a challenge concerning moving the business forward. Business plans and personal development plans will result from the CEO challenge. It is acknowledged that CEOs need to improve their business diagnostics and think more as business-people than as PR practitioners. This part of the development programme will be run by Development Associates, part of Deloitte & Touche.

CEO appraisals

In the UK, CEO and divisional head appraisals will be carried out by Philip Dewhurst, chief executive UK. Director appraisals will be carried out by CEOs.

Performance measures are set against four 'cornerstones', which are success criteria for the business:

1. distinctive business proposition;

2. client relationships;

3. superb financial performance;

4. great place to work.

New director development programme – the 1,000-day plan

The three elements in the new programme are:

1. strategy;

2. finance for non-financial directors – theory and Shandwick practice;

3. people – practical dealings with motivating people, influencing people to do what is required, poor performers and so on, all supported by theory such as Maslow.

The course provides a framework, and then specifics are added on as appropriate for different practice groups or roles. Course content is provided online, because directors from all over the world are involved, making a single location impractical. The online system provides for cross-team and cross-country working. The 'Shandwick Knowledge-base' is a group-wide intranet, which includes case studies. Participants are given pre-course work and all courses are biased towards live issues with help to work through to solutions. Internal communication of strategy and business status is carried out formally and regularly by a group of 'ambassadors'.

(Source: interview with Liz Nottingham on 28 February 2000.)

CASE 7 – 3i

Key issues

This case examines a recruitment, placement, development and net-working programme for independent directors placed by a venture capital company as non-executive directors on the boards of the companies in which it invests to represent its interests and help enhance their value.

Introduction

3i invests to help boards realize their plans to grow their businesses. It provides a mixture of equity and loan capital tailored to fit each company's needs – whether it is an existing business that wants to expand, or a management buy-out, buy-in or start-up. The company is Europe's leading venture capital company and has a network of over 30 offices in Europe, Asia Pacific and the United States. 3i has invested almost £11 billion in over 13,000 businesses and currently has a portfolio of over 3,000 companies with a combined valuation of £4.5 billion.

Overview of independent director programme

3i is in the business of backing boards of directors who will enhance the value of its investment. It believes its investment is likely to be more successful if there is a strong board, including independent directors. Recognizing the special needs of these directors, 3i launched its independent director programme (IDP) in 1986. The programme was designed to bring companies together with suitably qualified independent directors. The programme has become the UK's leading placer of independent directors, with IDP members now on the boards of over 1200 3i backed businesses. It is also developing internationally. 3i coined the phrase 'independent director' because of its belief that a non-executive director should think independently. It looks for the following characteristics in members of its independent director programme:

- previous successful leadership of a management buy-out, management buy-in, start-up or other entrepreneurial team;

- successful experience as a chairman, managing director, chief executive or finance director;

- financial independence;

- strong interpersonal skills – people who can be challenging and constructive as well as good motivators;

- a keen sense of awareness of shareholder issues;

- genuine international experience.

In summary, the programme selects those who have been through what the teams 3i is backing are about to encounter. 3i want people who are sound in judgement and have an ability to influence others. Most matches are made on situational experience and not on 'template thinking'.

Application process

The IDP unit receives a strong flow of high-calibre candidates. The unit's aim is to balance supply and demand, so that being on the programme means there is a reasonable likelihood of an appointment. The mix of membership reflects the growing multinational mix of 3i's business. Potential candidates are asked to submit a CV and complete a formal application (you can see this on the 3i Web site: www.3i.com). Candidates then meet with the IDP unit and an investment team.

Following these interviews, references are taken. New members are provided with a welcome pack including 3i's menu-style appointment letter and other useful best practice material.

Best practice events and research

3i organizes quarterly events so that IDP members can get together, draw upon the experience of others and discuss best practice. Events are regularly held in the UK, Continental Europe and Asia Pacific. The events get a very high turn-out of members. Previous topics have included:

■ market leadership;

■ managing board disharmony;

■ internationalizing a business;

■ running board meetings.

The events use case studies for discussion and learning.

IDP also conducts research into independent director issues and regularly publishes information for members. An example is the annual joint survey with the Top Pay Research Group on independent directors' time commitment and remuneration. For example, in 1998 the Top Pay survey asked questions about the desirability of training and induction processes for newly appointed independent directors:

> Do you believe it is important that newly appointed independent directors should be offered formal training? Yes 54%. No 46%.

> And a formal introduction or induction to the business they are joining? Yes 98%. No 2%.

Inducting a new independent director

It is a challenging process to introduce a new independent director to a board or to form a fresh boardroom team for a new venture. Methodical selection is only the first ingredient for success. Rigorous and thoughtful letters of appointment, induction programmes and review mechanisms will increase the chance of an effective appointment. 3i has developed a menu-style appointment letter to cover these issues.

IDP online

IDP online is a Web site developed for the exclusive use of IDP members. The objective is to enable those on IDP to tap into the collective knowledge and connections of their peers as well as the staff of 3i. In addition, IDP online contains a wealth of other useful information for independent directors. Around 300 IDP members are already registered.

Issues

Issues include the following:

Internationalizing is the big challenge.

▌ There are significant differences in the nature of the role in different countries, but the similarities are greater.

▌ While the press focuses mainly on governance issues of independent directors, it is equally important to have someone who will help with decisions on strategy and resource.

▌ The programme avoids over-rampant entrepreneurs, as the control-freak tendency may be too strong.

▌ IDP appointments need not be long-term and directors should know when it's time to go.

'We all need a regular dose of real world calibration in order to prevent delusions of competence and CEOs are no different!' (Patrick Dunne, director, 3i plc).

(Source: information gained from interview with Patrick Dunne on 10 March 2000.)

CASE 8 – A SCHOOL GOVERNING BODY

Key issues

This case considers changes in the work of a school governing body following legislation and an Ofsted report, and shows how the training opportunities set up by the governors themselves, the school and the local education and diocesan authorities helped to meet the needs that arose.

Introduction

This case study presents the personal impressions of one governor and may not represent the view of the governing body as a whole. The author joined the school's governing body in 1990, was elected vice-chair in 1992 and served 18 months as chair from 1997 to 1998. The legislation that transformed school governing bodies into legal boards came into being in early 1991 when this school had a pilot year of LMS (local management of schools).

The school is a three-form entry, inner-city, girls secondary school. It is a voluntary-aided Church of England foundation, funded through the local authority. It is growing in popularity, which means competition for places is fierce. It is also growing in numbers – from three-form entry (99 pupils) to four-form (120 pupils). The sixth form is also growing in numbers and popularity.

A governing body's duties

Parliament has given a range of duties and powers to governing bodies under the Education Acts. In brief, they include the following:

- conducting the school with a view to promoting high standards of educational achievement;

- setting appropriate targets for pupil achievement;

- taking general responsibility for the conduct of the school in broad strategic terms;

- managing the school's budget;

- making sure that the curriculum for the school is balanced and broadly based;

- determining the staff complement and a pay policy for the school;

▌ appointing the headteacher, deputy headteacher and other staff, and regulating staff conduct and discipline;

▌ drawing up an action plan after an inspection.

The challenges the governing body in this school has faced are:

▌ board composition;

▌ board development;

▌ individual governor training.

Board composition

There are 23 governors, which is an unpaid position. Various interested bodies appoint governors: the foundation governors come from within the Anglican Church and outnumber the representative governors from the local authority, staff, parents and local community. Owing to changes in the legislation, the balance of representation on the governing body had to be changed. As the number of parent representatives had to be increased from two to six, the local authority representation went down from four to two. Changing the balance from the old requirements to the new was a challenge. The headteacher is a governor and the deputy heads attend full governing body meetings. Heads of departments attend committee meetings as appropriate. It has become necessary for the governing body to seek specific skills, for example legal or financial knowledge.

Board development

With its new legal status, the board had to put a number of demanding procedures into place:

▌ A school mission statement was agreed. The first two of its seven aims are: 'We help and enable pupils to: develop lively, enquiring minds and the ability to question and argue rationally; acquire knowledge and skills relevant to adult life and employment in a fast changing world'.

▌ The school's management plan was developed as a management tool with financial implications. The governors receive a substantial document before the particular meeting at which it is the main focus, and discuss it in detail. It covers the major areas of:

- school policy, for example the library and the curriculum;

- departmental plans, for example design and technology, and the business studies faculty;

- financial summary, which outlines the requests for finance in the management plan and the allocations to curriculum areas and departments. Every department has a substantial input into the draft plan and the whole school consults with the governors. To get financial backing, any activity must be included in the plan and the governors must agree it and include it in the final plan.

▌ There are two main governing body meetings a term when the work of the governors and committees is integrated. Other committees meet either monthly or as appropriate.

▌ Targets for the school, both academic and 'business', are set by the governing body in line with guidelines. The governing body also manages the budget. One of the main governors' targets is to keep up with legislation. There can be additional money attached to the implementation of new ways of working. The training of staff is now part of the budget and governors' management plans.

Board development was formally initiated after an Ofsted report in 1994. The board had to find ways of rectifying the deficiencies found in the school. The issues were mainly around raising the standard of teaching. Some of the processes put into place were:

▌ The governing body supported the headteacher in reorganizing the staffing structure of the school.

▌ The governors became more knowledgeable about the school by spending time in the school.

▌ Governors joined interviewing panels for staff appointments.

▌ Governors started observing lessons.

▌ The governing body was restructured so that each governor took on an aspect of the school work, for example a subject area, or health and safety.

▪ The staff spent time making presentations to the governors, attending Saturday morning joint training sessions and serving on committees. This improved the informal relationships between the staff and governors and also increased the governors' knowledge of the school.

▪ The 'governor of the week' went into school and 'shadowed' girls in the school.

The governing body's main task is assessment and monitoring of all aspects of the school. It gets on well together and is able to cope with silences and awkward questions.

Individual governor training

It has been found that it takes about three years to train a governor fully. There are considerable training opportunities available on topics such as admissions, exclusions, teachers' pay, discipline of pupils and staff, redundancy, health and safety, staffing procedures, finance and budgeting, Ofsted, the governing body's structure and processes.

Courses are run by the local authority and the diocesan board of education, who also circulate helpful documents and induction packs. The local authority arranges meetings for the chairs of governing bodies to discuss specific issues. The DfEE provides pertinent information especially *'Guide to the Law for School Governors'*, (2000). Spending time in school is part of governor development. Members of the staff present training on ongoing topics such as exclusions and the curriculum. The school holds an annual joint governors–staff training meeting on a selected topic.

As being a governor is an unpaid activity, individuals differ in the time they can commit to training and attendance at meetings. This can be a problem for the governing body, but is not a major impediment.

CASE 9 – NHS SOUTH WEST BOARD

Key issues

This case discusses the transformation of the management structure and boards involving over 50 newly created semi-autonomous organizations. Key issues are the development of the chair and all the roles in the board, and in particular the selection and appraisal of non-executive directors.

Introduction

The NHS is the largest employer in Europe. From 1948–1985, NHS organizations were managed by triumvirates. Arguably so that no one was in charge and administration rather than leadership was valued. The Griffiths Report in 1983 recommended vast changes to the NHS, including the appointment of general managers. In the next few years the first NHS personnel director and over 800 executives were recruited.

A major reorganization in 1990 prepared the way for semi-autonomous organizations, which would either purchase or provide services. Each had its own board. The internal market was designed to separate out responsibilities and provide greater incentive to improve services and value for money. Arguably there were no non-executive or executive directors in the NHS at that time. Chairs and non-executive directors were appointed to the boards by the secretary of state, usually based on networking, ie they were known locally. Following appointment there was no formal development. People just got on with it, and were believed to be able to transfer skills from one sector to another and one organization to another. A significant percentage of males were appointed.

Janet Trotter, chief executive of Cheltenham and Gloucester College of Higher Education (CGCHE), was appointed the non-executive chair of Gloucestershire Health in 1992 and subsequently the non-executive chair of the NHS Executive South West in 1996. Her responsibilities include nominating individuals to the secretary of state for appointment to the 50 NHS authorities and boards in the South West Region. She has also increasingly taken a keen interest in the development of chairs and non-executive directors so that boards function as effectively and efficiently as possible.

Context for change

The changes envisaged in the NHS in 1990 were formidable and it was intended that the reality of the internal market would be effective within three years. Some of the organizations were handling £200–300 million per year. At this time there were over 50 chairs of the various boards in the South West Region, over 220 non-executive directors, over 50 chief executives and over 220 executive directors.

The appointment process became a key area of focus. It was clear that improvements were needed in the selection of board members. Also, more open processes were needed to ensure greater accountability, diversity and transparency for local people. The HR director of the NHS Executive South West provided two names for each chair vacancy to the minister responsible. The process involved sifting and interview by a senior member of the regional office staff, an independent assessor and Janet Trotter herself.

The non-executive directors were selected in a similar way. The criteria for all roles were laid down for the secretary of state and key among these was involvement in the local community and commitment to public service.

Board development

Each board normally comprises the chair, five non-executive directors and five executive directors (chief executive, plus typically finance, corporate affairs, medical and human resources).

At the appointment phase, effort was taken to nominate individuals for non-executive director appointment who would provide balance (skills, gender and ethnicity) and be able to add value to the organization in its journey. Nevertheless, Janet Trotter realized that individuals needed training and support if they were to maximize their contribution within the context of the NHS, which is a large, complex and dynamic organization.

Following consultation with chairs, a framework for development was put together comprising three elements:

1. *Induction.* This included local events designed to introduce the non-executive director to key staff and partners and to board business. Regional activities focused primarily on bringing non-executive directors up to a good level of understanding of NHS issues and of their own roles.

2. *Ongoing development.* This aspect of development was organized primarily so that individuals could be kept up to speed with the modernization agenda in the NHS.

3. *Thematic or functional development.* This strand was primarily to develop non-executive directors in their various roles: complaints convenor, mental health act management, audit committee member. This included open-ended development such as bringing together all the chairs of audit committees to review current issues and best practice, and to ensure effective management of audit business.

Helping chairs to develop their skills and support them in creating healthy boards was a further concern, and a specific training and development programme was designed, again in consultation, to support them in their work. This had three elements:

1. *Induction.* Each new chair had induction by the regional chair and was then assigned an experienced chair within the region as a mentor. After six months the newly appointed chair undertook a self-assessment supported by the mentor. This was shared with the regional chair and agreed as a basis for the new chair's further development. A formal appraisal took place after 18 months.

2. *Ongoing development.* This entailed meetings with Janet Trotter every two months to keep local chairs abreast of developments in the NHS and of key priorities.

3. *Thematic or functional development.* This was designed to enhance the effectiveness of chairs and involved a range of activities such as chairing board meetings, dealing with the media and handling the relationship with the chief executive (perhaps the most vital in each organization).

The training and development programme was begun in 1997. All chairs and non-executive directors were involved. Two-way feedback was improved in 1997, when appraisals of all non-executive directors and chairs were introduced to provide regular review against agreed objectives, and to support nominations for reappointment or otherwise. The chair of each authority or trust appraised non-executive directors annually. Reports were sent to Janet Trotter who then appraised the performance of each chair. The chair appraised the chief executive and together they appraised the members of the executive team.

Given the significant changes to NHS structures in the late 1990s and the creation of the first primary care trusts (PCTs), with their own boards, in 2000, Janet Trotter considered whether it was possible to provide specific development for non-executive directors who might wish to be chairs of PCTs, trusts or authorities in future, thus addressing concerns about succession planning and development.

In 2000, via the appraisal process, a group of non-executives was invited to take part in a learning set (10 were held across the region) led by an experienced chair and with a set agenda involving case study work. Both chairs and non-executive directors valued this small group work, which focused on helping participants understand more about NHS organizations and how they work, and on the key responsibilities of the chair and board. So successful have these learning sets been that consideration is being given to providing similar sessions for all non-executive directors. Boards also have away days to consider strategic direction and to deal with specific issues related to their health community.

Janet Trotter has an education and training background, and the programme has primarily been developed and run by her and her staff, with specialists being used as additional resources as required. Additionally, chairs have led sessions and contributed from their experience and these sessions have been particularly valued.

Measurements

A simple measurement of the effectiveness of these programmes is whether boards delivered their objectives, for example health improvement of a local population, waiting list target, management of winter pressures and financial balance. These were assessed by performance tables and annual review.

Softer measurement is in the way each board managed its business and its relationships, both internally and with local partners and the media. Additionally, non-executive directors and chairs are encouraged to contribute to ongoing evaluations of the training and development programme and to offer proposals for improvement.

Achievements

Most chairs believed in training and development at board level. Most boards understood the pace of change in the NHS and the pace required of them. Most of those involved appreciated the significance of the chair/chief executive relationship and the need for boards to be welded together to perform effectively.

It is self-evident that the best performing organizations have the best leadership. A seminar with chairs listed the qualities necessary of a chair as open, challenging, responsible, visible, drawing all people in the NHS together and making them feel valued, and leadership through the team.

Issues for the future

Human resource issues will move further up the NHS agenda, for example tackling poor performance, promoting diversity and assuring equality. It is the workforce that will improve the quality of services, provide improved patient care and user support and modernize the NHS: people are the key to the future. Boards, therefore, have a key role to play in setting the tone and style of the NHS locally and in taking the agenda forward, and their training will need to match that of the workforce.

(Sources: first draft based on telephone interview with Janet Trotter, HR director, NHS Executive South West, and chief executive of CGCHE, on 22 May 2000; draft revised by Janet Trotter on 26 June 2000.)

CASE 10 – OXFAM GB

Introduction

Oxfam GB's purpose is to work with others to overcome poverty and suffering. Affiliated to Oxfam International, Oxfam GB in the 1998/99 financial year had a turnover of £124.3m. Employees total 3700 whilst there are 21000+ volunteers around the country.

The current Director, David Bryer, was appointed in 1992. He inherited a structured, hierarchical and compartmentalized organization and was faced with the need to streamline the organization to establish direction, satisfy stakeholders and ensure appropriate governance of the agency. Decision making was unclear with decisions being batted to and fro between Trustees, management and sixteen sub-committees.

Driven by the recession and the need to be more professional and strategic to compete with other charities for funds, a strategic intent was developed in 1993 by corporate management and a group of trustees. The result was a clear plan of action but through a process that was top down and exclusive. By 1996, despite greater clarity of purpose, more effective fundraising and a range of good programmes overseas, Oxfam faced a logjam in its ways of working.

In spite of there being a more coherent vision and a raft of supporting guidelines, procedures and policies, there was still the feeling that this model was limited at a time when the leadership of the organization needed to be nimble, innovative and challenging in response to the differing and potentially divergent needs of the various stakeholders in order to retain their commitment and support.

In short, it was felt that the following was needed:

▪ one culture and an agreed set of values to focus the energy and commitment;

▪ strategic leadership able to adjust in the light of organizational performance and changing external circumstances;

▪ inclusiveness both within Oxfam and externally across public, private and non-government sectors to keep the various stakeholders involved;

▪ corporate centre to add value in a leadership model which sets policy parameters, encourages innovation within strong systems of performance accountability.

Governance in the early 1990s

Until 1993, the legal and moral responsibilities of Oxfam were held by a council of some 60 trustees supported by 16 sub-committees. The composition of the council was determined more by the need to reflect the diversity of stakeholder groups and to incorporate specific skills than to equip itself for a more strategic role

The corporate management team consisted of the director, managers of each of the main divisions and one for internal business support, ie finance and people. The organization was structured along corporate, hierarchical lines resulting in a silo mentality, resulting in a lack of teamwork with departments fighting their corner, with different perceptions on issues resulting in departments having different priorities.

The changes made

The external facilitator

Oxfam, perhaps like many charities was heavily governed and influenced by values and perception. ' It was a passionate, cerebral organization – not great on management skills.' Whereas this gave Oxfam a strength it also meant there was scope for great disagreement and potential for strategic drift. The first element of the change process was to appoint an external consultant for two years (subsequently extended one further year) to work with the council and the corporate management team. She started with a fact-based analysis of the organization to start to confront some of the differing perceptions that were blocking change and effectiveness. The remit was to review where the organization was going, recommend mechanisms to improve governance of the charity and to instigate stakeholder surveys to improve communication, consultation and ownership.

The benefits of having a full time consultant on board was summarized as creating the step change the leadership felt was needed to align behaviours to the way the organization was heading. Defining the culture, introducing behavioural competences, using them to redefine the organization would probably have happened in 'a logical processy way' but not in the time or the depth that happened in the late 1990s. Furthermore through mentoring the chair of council and director, the consultant facilitated role definition enabling greater robustness and challenge so enhancing the partnership.

Streamlining governance

The governance of Oxfam was too unwieldy making the decision-making process too cumbersome and effectively distracting the council from their real purpose of providing direction to the organization. The trustees were too dysfunctional with no clear collective objectives.

In a two-stage process, the size of the council was reduced first from 60 to 25 and then in 1998 to 12 people, the emphasis being not on stakeholder representation, for this was addressed elsewhere, (discussed later) or having the right names on the letterhead, but on having the complementary skills to effectively lead a £100m+ organization. The emphasis on governance was then to be on setting strategy, agreeing strategic objectives, approving the allocation of resources and monitoring performance.

Trustees are appointed for 3 years renewable for a further 3 on re-selection. Selection and / or reselection is based much more now on clearly specified criteria including team balance both in terms of views and style.

The benefits derived from a smaller council allowed more rational discussion and debate providing greater clarity on the agenda and empowerment to make real decisions against the criteria listed above. The consultant would observe the dynamics of council meetings to ensure that they were focusing on the issues – including diversity and inclusiveness.

Professionalizing management

Although the corporate management team (CMT) would be marginally increased it was argued that professional finance and human resource professionals were needed. Finance and HR directors were recruited. Assessment centre methodologies began to be used for all senior and strategic posts, not so much to ensure technical competence but that individual personal values and styles of working fitted the culture of the organization moving forwards.

This fitted with a general desire to improve the calibre of management throughout the organization by focusing on behavioural competences and so start to begin a process of focusing on how things were done rather than solely on what was achieved essential though that was.

This was supported by the fact that the consultant sat in on most of the management meetings to comment on the way the management team behaved and the degree to which the team stayed true to its objectives. By having a smaller council increasingly focused on strategic leadership, the corporate management team's relationship to them changed to a more robust partnership. One example of this is the fact that the CMT agree objectives and identify key behavioural competencies for the team as a whole with the trustees annually. The relationship between the trustees and the CMT moved away from a destructive adversarial one to that of partnership and challenge.

Maintaining the momentum

Having a team / individual coach might be regarded as both a luxury and a danger in creating an undesirable dependence. How have the council, management team and director created processes to avoid slippage back into the old ways?

The council have formal process reviews at the end of their regular meetings to see if they are fulfilling their objectives. Recently they looked at their agendas for the previous year to see if meetings were becoming institutionalized. The selection process is more robust. Greater emphasis is held on the council seeing more of each other than at the 6 formal meetings a year. Trustees are encouraged to attend the assembly (an annual meeting of about 200 stakeholders including trustees, CMT, donors, programme partners, staff, volunteers and guests from other Oxfam organizations). Retreats are arranged to consider, for example, the outcomes of the strategic review.

The trustees also have a day's induction on, in particular, Oxfam's expectations and responsibilities. The trustees are also encouraged to undertake visits to offices and projects overseas.

The corporate management team have been encouraged to work as a team particularly now with the emphasis on the means as well as the end. There is a greater feeling that any dysfunctionality of views and behaviour can be discussed and dealt with. Recently, all the team attended a 3 day strategic leadership programme designed to develop performance management as part of an initiative for the top 200 managers in Oxfam. The team is encouraged to attend follow up modules as part of a refocused training programme. The next main module is on delivering cost-effectiveness.

On a one-to-one basis, the director works with the individual CMT member on their individual needs in relation to competence development. The director himself is monitored by the chair and is partially mentored by the finance and HR directors. In the present environment, it is probably rare to know that your role will last as long as 10 years let alone knowing that there is a finite time period. One attribute of a successful director appears to be the desire to be stretched and constantly challenged through constant change, being invited to do more things and, perhaps uniquely, having an external mentor who both acted as a catalyst for change and acted as a mentor.

Succession Planning

Development has become a management tool during the 1990's – no more so than in planning for succession. New people had to be brought in from outside to professionalize the CMT in the early 1990s. It is now an expectation that 50 per cent of a future CMT should be grown from within. Key people within are being developed and groomed for the future – taking advantage of public development programmes but also a view by the director that there should be potential successors to the role from within. So one director has been given the role of Oxfam's representative in India as one such development move. Conscious thought has been given to activities/experiences that individuals at the top of the organization might do to put themselves in the frame for director roles.

Trustees may be in post for 6 years. Their replacement will usually come from within the organization, to the extent that one of the criteria for selection is that they must have had some association with Oxfam prior to being put forward. This policy reiterates the philosophy that selection is then based on a person's skills and contribution and how they would complement the trustee team rather than the fact that they are chief executive of a well-known company, which will somehow translate into an effective contribution to the organization.

Lessons learned

1.   The importance of getting governance right and clarifying roles.

2.   Getting the relationship between corporate management and the trustees right. In particular this has meant the trustees focusing on providing strategic leadership and not getting bogged down by the weight of operational detail. It also meant getting to know each other and growing professional respect for each other and avoiding the situation where trustees might be peripheral to the business. This was done by getting trustees and corporate management to work jointly on the strategy. Trustee meetings were broken up by meal breaks to allow time for everyone to get to know each other as people and maximize the opportunities for continuing to develop relationships. By clarifying roles and building this personal relationship, expectations were raised to the extent that second rate submissions for approval were thrown back to the author for revision and improvement.

3.   The importance of getting the relationship between the director and the chair right. It is planned that in 2001 Oxfam would appoint the director first and then – from the remaining trustees – appoint the chair that best complemented the different strengths.

4.   Concentrate on the ways of working as well as the jobs to be done. The competences clearly support the desired culture. One example

of this in practice is that senior managers, including CMT, will be piloting 360 degree feedback as part of the performance management system.

5.   Throughout the transformation process keep focusing on the external market, change a few key people if possible and ensure that you create enough of a critical mass of people who want change (50–60 in this case).

(Sources: Conversations with the Oxfam Director, David Bryer, 17 March 2000 and subsequent paper review/amendment and further conversation 24 October 2000. Conversation with Jane Cotton – HR Director. Excerpts from Oxfam GB Strategic Review, 1998)

CASE 11 – ACTION LEARNING

Introduction

In 1994, as a result of IoD Diploma holders asking 'What next?', staff at Leeds Metropolitan University Business School developed a Master's degree for directors. They aimed to provide an innovative and challenging learning experience, which would be both theoretical and practical, with learning firmly rooted in the complex realities of participants' businesses. They were particularly anxious that the directors on the course gained business, as well as personal, benefits. To this end they incorporated a number of opportunities for participants to choose what they wanted to learn, alongside the formal taught programme. The culmination of the course was the Action Learning Project.

Action Learning

Reg Revans (1984) formulated the idea of action learning in the 1940s. Since then it has been used by a wide range of companies. It encompasses four main elements:

z a problem or issue that is important to the company, to which there are no obvious solutions;

▪ someone who has the authority to do something about it and take action;

▪ someone who is willing to take a risk to develop themselves and their company;

▪ a system for learning reflectively, the set, in which in Revans terms 'comrades in adversity' freely question, challenge and support, and learn from each other.

The directors participating in the programme brought the first three elements, whilst business school staff brought their knowledge and experience of action learning in practice.

Starting out

On the first two days the directors were introduced to the ideas of action learning, and formed themselves into sets of four or five people. At this stage they helped each other to think through the issues or problems that were crucial for their companies, and consider which might form the basis of their project. Initial ideas were agreed, and the set contracted to meet for a number of days over the following six to eight months. In practice most sets met between four and six times during this period, and each set had a facilitator from the University. Although the majority of sets met at the venue where their taught modules had taken place (Leeds, Wakefield or London), two sets made the decision to have a set meeting at each of their companies. This proved to be an added bonus when trying to understand the context and complexities that surrounded each individual's selected issue.

The role of the facilitator was to act as a process consultant, encouraging the questioning and reflective behaviours that contribute so successfully to the problem-solving process. They did not provide expert help on the specific projects.

The problems and issues addressed

Projects included:

▪ starting a new business;

▪ building the top team;

▋ improving effectiveness and efficiency in the procurement department of a large shipbuilding and repair yard;

▋ developing a marketing strategy;

▋ acquisitions and mergers;

▋ intellectual capital and brand in the business;

▋ relocation of the business.

The activities

At each set meeting each director has at least one hour to tell the story of their problem to date. The job of their fellow directors in the set is to listen and then to ask questions. Questions are the keys to reflection and learning, not advice. The tempting 'If I were you I would . . .' is discouraged. The contention is that the person with the problem knows more about its context and nature than anyone else ever can. They are the experts and have to come to their own understanding and decisions about what should be done. High-quality questioning aids individual reflection and helps people see the problem from a different perspective. It can help redefine the issue, enable them to see their part in what is happening, and clarify why things are happening the way they are and what action needs to be taken next.

Between set meetings delegates carry out their action plans. These can cover actions required within the company, together with activities to meet the learning requirements. These include gathering information from other companies and the industry, reading relevant academic and business literature and utilizing and supplementing the formal learning from the Master's programme. Participants are also encouraged to keep written reflective logs on their actions and the thoughts and feelings that accompany what they are doing.

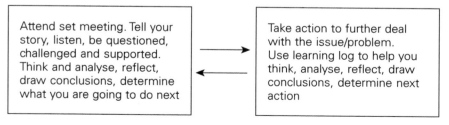

Figure 9.2 *The action learning project*

The gains

For the directors the results of this process are not always what are expected or indeed comfortable, but for the majority this is a strong learning experience.

> *The set's constructive questioning led me to ask myself whether it was necessary for the business to remain in processing in order to achieve its long-term goals. This was a radical departure from the company's current thinking, which saw manufacture as its raison d'être even though its expansion plans were in food service . . . I explored areas that were previously unthinkable . . . and saw my situation from new and different perspectives.*

The same director comments:

> *What I gave to other set members and received back in full measure, was challenging questions that shook the whole structure of self belief . . . The result of these challenges to some of their basic assumptions was a journey of self discovery and awareness that change their whole perspective on their lives and business. This enabled them to remove blockages and problems that emanated from them but which they previously had been blind to.*

And from other directors:

> *I have reflected on where I have learned most. Undoubtedly it has been from the set meetings. The absolute honesty, politic free constructive criticism has been invaluable. However, I did find some of the comments made that challenged my views sometimes a little unpalatable, although usually correct.*

> *Undertaking this work provided me with a multi-dimensional, intense learning experience I had not expected. Most of the time I found it challenging, exciting and rewarding, but there were moments when I found it almost surreal and thought I might end up on the psychiatrist's couch . . . I am conscious of having undergone a profound learning experience in gaining a better understanding of the learning process and how to harness its power both for the company's and my personal development.*

> *Being in the set with people like me who I could trust and open up to was a godsend. It was OK not to always have the answers and to admit sometimes that I didn't know.*

In brief, directors have learned:

▪ greater skills in posing relevant questions, listening, reflection, making connections, exploring options, analysis and decision making;

▪ increased awareness of themselves and their impact on others;

▪ increased self confidence;

▪ the importance of peer support, peer learning and networking;

▪ how to learn from their own and other people's experiences and mistakes.

This learning has translated into real change within their companies and the impact of action learning has been such that a number have introduced problem solving through action learning within their own companies.

(Source: Judith Barras, November 2000)

10

The future for the board

Bernard Taylor, Philip Stiles and Mahen Tampoe

INTRODUCTION

In the earlier parts of this book you have already considered the speed of change in the business environment and the need for the board to achieve strategic flexibility. In this chapter we present an abbreviated report of a Delphi study on the future of the board – in essence, an attempt to provide a new agenda for British boards of directors.

THE DELPHI METHOD

A Delphi survey is in four phases:

1. *planning*: work with a small group of specialists to list the topics, design and pilot-test the questionnaire and identify a group of experts;

2. *survey and analysis*: distribute the questionnaire and analyse the results;

3. *feedback*: communicate the results to the experts for clarification and make amendments to the questionnaire;

4. *second survey*: conduct a second survey to enable members of the group to take account of new ideas and to have second thoughts.

The second survey usually produces greater consensus and a clearer picture.

The technique is particularly helpful where there is insufficient data for trend analysis and where the future is uncertain. The idea is to gather the opinions of a number of experts and to avoid the personality conflicts that can arise in a face-to-face meeting where a few articulate individuals can dominate the discussion.

THE STUDY

The British working party on the future role of the board carried out the study for the Centre for Organisational Studies (COS) based in Barcelona. The aim of the working party was to promote a dialogue about the future of corporate governance in general, and the changing role of boards of directors in particular. The specific goals were to identify important trends and events that might impact on the development of boards of directors, and to predict how and when these might occur.

The final list of 73 questions was divided into seven categories: membership of the board; reports to shareholders; employment of directors; regulation and litigation; improving board effectiveness; key trends affecting boards, and barriers to reform.

THE RESULTS

Based on the responses to our questions we can make the following predictions about the main boards of British quoted companies:

■ The boards of companies will undergo frequent systematic self-assessment.

▌ The performance of individual directors will be evaluated on a regular basis.

▌ The performance of the CEO will also be evaluated periodically.

▌ Directors will not be required to have professional qualifications in direction as a condition of their appointment.

▌ Companies operating with a unitary board system will split the roles of chairman and chief executive, if they have not already done so.

▌ Institutional investors will be obliged to use their votes at annual general meetings.

▌ Companies in the UK will not see a large increase in the number of women or foreign nationals on their boards.

▌ Written guidelines for corporate governance practice will become commonplace.

▌ Retired CEOs and executive directors will be required to resign from the board.

▌ UK companies will follow the US trend and pay non-executive directors partly in shares.

The experts identified three major challenges for boards over the next five years:

1. *Board composition.* In order to compete successfully in rapidly changing world markets, companies need to use their recruitment and selection policies to build more diverse boards of directors.

2. *Improving board performance.* Companies need a greater focus on making boards more effective.

3. *Converging cultures.* Corporate governance in Britain may move towards an international or US model but experts were much more cautious on this issue.

Board composition

Two issues arose. First, the Cadbury Report (1992) had highlighted the need for boards to have 'independent' non-executive directors. Independence was defined as not having previously been employed by the company nor having received any other fees. The experts identified this balance of inside and outside directors as one of the major influences when shortcomings in board performance have been studied. The issue is whether the CEO and executive directors are matched by the non-executives. Their concern was the potential shortfall of non-executives. The increasing pressure on existing executive directors might inhibit them from taking on non-executive directorships. On the other hand, experts thought that the shortfall would be made up by an increasing number of CEOs and executives who would resign late in their careers and take on portfolios of non-executive directorships.

A second major issue concerning board composition was the separation of the roles of chairman and chief executive. The dangers of one person taking both roles were an unhealthy concentration of power, a conflict of interests, opportunistic behaviour and a possible reduction of shareholder wealth. The CEO might also be tempted to groom a successor in his or her own image. Some organization theorists argue that, for the purposes of strategy formation, organizations should be led by strong CEOs with clear lines of authority. Such leadership may also send positive signals to shareholders that there is a clear sense of direction in the company, which may confer legitimacy on the firm.

In our study, respondents were clear that the split was a positive step in ensuring good governance, not only for large companies but also for small and medium-sized enterprises. However, one chief executive who is also the chairman of his company stressed that splitting the roles should not be made mandatory.

Board representation

Board representation is about the extent to which women, ethnic minorities and foreign nationals are found in the boardroom. This is one of the most contentious issues in corporate governance. Research undertaken by Sundridge Park (PA Consultancy, 1994) shone an illuminating light on the continuing under-representation of women at board level, as illustrated in Table 10.1.

Women are under-represented not only at board level but also in senior managerial positions. In 2000, there was only one female CEO

Table 10.1 *Characteristics of UK directors*

Characteristics	%
Age: over 50	75
Sex: male	96
Born in the UK	90
Attended public school	43
Attended Oxbridge	20
No public sector experience	83
No international experience	74
Holding other directorships	61
Career primarily in one organization	32

of a FTSE 100 company – Marjorie Scardino at Pearson plc – and figures overall do not look encouraging. Table 10.2 shows companies with (at least) one woman on the board in 1997; Table 10.3 shows the percentage of females on company boards, and Table 10.4 shows the percentage of females on NHS trust boards (Conyou and Mallin, 1997).

These tables confirm that women who do make it to board level are more likely to do so with backgrounds in the public services or the not-for-profit sector rather than in commercial life. In Europe, the picture is much the same, as shown in Table 10.5 (Korn Ferry International, 1996: 14).

Table 10.2 *Companies with (at least) one woman on the board (1997)*

	Number	Average Size of Board	Total Directors
FTSE 100	40	12	1,200
FTSE 350	73	10	3,500

Table 10.3 *Females on the board*

	Non-executives	Executives
FTSE 100	3.1%	0.6%
FTSE 350	2.0%	0.5%

Table 10.4 *Females on NHS trust boards*

	Non-executives	Executives
% Females	27.9%	31.5%

In one survey of 1,800 firms, only 17 per cent of chairmen had actively sought to appoint a woman non-executive, usually on the grounds that many of their customers were women or that having a woman on the board was socially and politically desirable. The results of our survey show that women continue to be under-represented, and respondents were pessimistic about the prospects for improvements in this area over the next five years.

Table 10.5 *Women on European boards*

Country	Type of Board	Percentage of Women Board Members
UK	unitary	5%
Germany	management	1%
	supervisory	5%
Northern Europe	management	6%
	supervisory	5%
France/Belgium	unitary/management	5%
	supervisory	9%

Similarly disappointing results were found with foreign nationals on the board. Directors now need to have experience of international markets and individual country cultures and contexts, but very little attention has been paid to the role of the board in managing across borders.

The major route to increasing international awareness is to appoint foreign nationals, usually as non-executive directors. They can also bring experience of particular local country conditions. A survey of Europe's largest 5,000 companies showed that 38 per cent of UK and other European boards have a foreign national director. The results from our survey show that despite increasing concerns about globalization, and a growing interconnection of markets and corporations, this figure is unlikely to increase.

Improving board performance

This study sought to gather opinions on how best boards might increase their own effectiveness and, by implication, the effectiveness of the organization as a whole. A number of issues emerged as key:

▌ self-assessment;

▌ director training;

▌ IT in the boardroom.

We shall take each in turn.

Self-assessment

Without critical self-analysis, problems can occur in the dynamics and performance of the board, yet many boards fail to evaluate their own performance. Companies that do undergo such a process usually employ a number of informal checks rather than any hard metrics.

Compare the following two examples. At one leading UK company, an annual review of board processes and practices is conducted by a leading non-executive, who interviews every board member informally to ask whether there is any area that can be improved. At another, a chairman's advisory committee examines the overall performance of the board and its committees. Its clarification of accountabilities and its assessment of directors' contributions enhance the board's evaluation and control role. They also allow board norms to be uncovered and examined. The committee provides a further opportunity to analyse the skill mix and the size of the board, and determine whether any new directors need to be selected or whether any incumbents should be retired. For both individual directors, and the board as a whole, this mechanism was thought to be very important.

Director training

Many studies have documented the low level of take-up of director courses in the UK. The reasons include the unattractiveness of the content or the framing of the course, the unwillingness of directors to admit to needing training, and lack of time for training. It is still surprising, given the emphasis on continuous transformation and the learning organization, that many directors consider themselves exempt from this process. According to a survey by Norman Broadbent, the main training and development opportunities continue to be business school courses, but individual coaching and mentoring are being emphasized as more effective ways of increasing capability. The notion of introducing a formal qualification for directors, as a condition for appointment, was not well received.

IT in the boardroom

The increasing use of information technology in the boardroom might help to reduce the information disadvantage suffered by non-executives and speed the flow of knowledge to the whole board. It would also help to improve communication between the board and the share-holders/stakeholders, particularly small shareholders who could access information about the company relatively cheaply. Greater use of video-conferencing to link up to overseas operations is another important way forward. However, as one expert said: 'Don't underestimate the value and importance of the personal visit, for motivation, and collecting self-knowledge and environmental awareness'.

Other issues that emerged from the study were for directors to have independent advice about research into new technologies and new markets from management consultants, advisory boards of scientists and technologists, and international specialists. To keep them up to date, the experts have suggested boards of large companies form strategy committees to help weigh strategic proposals.

Converging cultures

There was keen debate among our respondents on the notion of international convergence. Traditionally, two models of governance have been identified as dominant forms: 1) the US/UK model, which emphasizes high liquidity in capital markets and a market for corporate control by take-over bids; and 2) the Continental model, which features prominently in Germany and Japan and is characterized by less liquid financial markets and a concentration of shareholder power in banks, families and governments. These models used to be seen as conflicting, but with increasing globalization, the development of worldwide capital markets and rapid information flows, there is now a prospect of convergence. As John Kay (1993: 66) states: 'Today we see different national models of corporate governance, but firms in a single region operate, in the main, in similar ways. Tomorrow we can expect fewer national differences but more variety in the matching of organisational structure to the requirements of different markets and industries'.

The idea of convergence is being driven by a number of forces. One is the fact that many Continental European countries have underfunded pension schemes. Fewer than one in four working people in the European Union is currently covered by a funded pension scheme, and as Price Waterhouse (1997) argue: 'the need to shift the burden of pension liabilities away from the state into the private sector is urgent'.

In future we could see a greater percentage of funds going into equities, with the result that shareholder value is likely to become a major consideration for European companies. Investors can now operate on a worldwide basis. Their decisions on investments will be affected both by the degree of openness offered by companies and the yield they can expect. Such concerns would work against companies in Japan and Germany, where the shareholder's voice is muted and financial disclosure has a mixed track record. At the same time, the short-termism that dogs UK and US systems of governance may be altered by the formation of long-term relationships between investors and companies in the style of Japanese/German governance. Their concern for employees will also be seen to be increasingly significant.

In terms of convergence, the UK is well placed as a result of its relatively high degree of transparency and delivery of shareholder value. There seems little value in trying to impose overarching governance frameworks on different national and cultural structures. Institutional investors, in particular, will have to expand their knowledge of different cultures and systems of governance, and ensure that they continue to talk with the key decision-makers within organizations.

At a macro level, governments should be wary of introducing too many governance prescriptions. Though this may increase confidence in the market, too much focus on compliance may make other markets more attractive for listing purposes.

The survey respondents were cautious on this issue. The implementation of the EU 5th Directive encouraging a two-tier structure for boards in the UK was dismissed by the experts, as was the idea of companies gaining a European registration by the European Union to simplify legal and fiscal complexities involved in running international business. But a number of respondents thought that increasing internationalization, through alliances and partnerships with joint boards and frequent meetings, would create a natural, informal move towards greater convergence. This would be in terms of processes and systems of regulation and reporting standards rather than board structure (unitary or two-tier). Many respondents also expected that companies would report on employee attitudes and employee satisfaction in their annual reports.

CONCLUSIONS

Our findings indicate that though Cadbury, Hampel and others have made for better corporate governance, there is still room for improvement. Much work has been concerned with improving accountability, but we have focused on the relatively neglected area of how boards can add value, and have cast an eye to the future to see what experts believe are the key factors for improving board performance. Two areas stood out – increasing board diversity and effectiveness – together with the use of IT, improvements in corporate reporting and a convergence of international trends.

Boards moving into the 21st century face strong challenges from an increasingly competitive and more global environment. In this chapter we have gone some way to showing what may change and what may not change in the future.

ACKNOWLEDGEMENTS

The authors wish to thank the following people for their generous support:

1. the Centre for Organisational Studies (COS), which initiated the project on the future for the board and allowed the draft report to be debated at their conference in October 1997;

2. the COS UK working party members, who helped to frame the questions, distributed the questionnaire and shaped the conclusions;

3. the Institute of Directors, which also distributed the questionnaire;

4. the 39 'experts in corporate governance' – leading directors, consultants and academics who kindly completed the Delphi questionnaire and gave their comments.

Appendix 1

Answers to the quiz

These are the reasons why each of the statements is false:

1. If the word 'director' is used on your business card you may, in certain circumstances, be considered to be holding yourself out as a director to other parties who may be dealing with you in good faith as a director even though you are not a member of the board. In certain circumstances you may have the same liabilities as board members. The term 'associate director' is used to describe senior executives without a seat on the board. Authority to use the term director should be provided for in the organization's constitution. Where the constitution permits the appointment of associate directors, the articles should specify the authority and power involved.

2. There is a difference between a chief executive and a managing director. The managing director is always a member of the board of directors but a chief executive officer is not necessarily a board member.

3. All members of the board have the same responsibility for determining financial strategy. Directors must ensure that internal control procedures are in place. In addition, they must obtain

reliable and valid information for monitoring the operations and performance of the organization. Refer to Chapter 2 for more detail.

4. Non-executive directors have, in general, the same responsibilities as executive directors. For example, the Companies Act does not distinguish between executive and non-executive directors. Refer to Chapter 2 for more detail.

5. It is safest to assume that directors of state-owned organizations including quangos, agencies, parastatals and schools are *not* exempt from normal directorial responsibilities. Even if limited by guarantee to £1, there are still situations where you are liable. Refer to Chapter 8 for more detail.

6. The concept of limited liability applies to shareholders, not directors. As a director of a limited company, your liabilities are normally unlimited. Refer to Chapter 3 for more detail.

7. The purpose and tasks of every board can be regarded as identical. These will be interpreted differently in different contexts. Refer to Chapter 1 for more detail.

8. Directors may be held to account by shareholders but in a limited company the prime responsibility of a director is to the company.

Appendix 2

IoD

The Institute of Directors has some 60,000 personal members and associates worldwide, including 50,000 in the UK, who have responsibility for the strategic direction of their companies. The Institute's motto is 'Integrity and Enterprise', and its mission is: 'to be the leading advocate for enterprise and job and wealth creation, by helping directors to fulfil their leadership responsibilities, for the benefit of business and society as a whole'. The IoD is strongly committed to raising directors' professional standards by encouraging directors to attain high levels of expertise and effectiveness and developing professional standards in boardroom practice. Below is a list of some of the courses and services offered by the IoD:

- **Courses for directors**: the IoD produce a range of over 30 short courses, (1, 2 and 3 day duration) formulated and developed from the directors viewpoint which are designed to be immediately relevant. They are led by business experts with outstanding experience in the facilitation of training. All of the courses provide an excellent opportunity to meet other directors and expand personal networks. Tel: (020) 7766 2606.

■ **Programmes for directors**: programmes of study are available form the IoD (9 and 15 day duration) including the Company Direction Programme which can lead to the award of a professionally recognized Diploma. Tel: (020) 7766 2606.

■ **Board Consultancy**: IoD Board consultancy offers services to main subsidiary and business unit boards from all types of organizations. The service helps boards to improve their structure, procedures and performance for enhanced corporate success – expertly delivered in the context of the organization's own industry, culture and addressing its key issues. Tel: (020) 7766 8802.

■ **Director conferences**: the IoD runs many one day conferences focusing on up-to-the-minute topics with speakers from many leading UK and international companies. The conferences offer a valuable learning experience and exposure to new ideas as well as excellent networking opportunities. Tel: (020) 7766 8938.

■ **Director coaching**: the IoD provide an executive coaching service that is available to deal with a range of personal and professional service. Tel: (020) 7766 2606.

■ **Books and publications**: a range of books and publications on director development issues are available from the IoD. Tel: (020) 7839 1233.

THE CHARTERED DIRECTOR

In 2000, a milestone was achieved in the UK when the Privy Council agreed to the creation of the chartered director qualification, the world's first professional standard specifically for directors. Chartered directors will be allowed to use the CDir designation. Admission to the chartered director profession is open to IoD members and fellows who satisfy all the requirements and subscribe to the Code of Professional Conduct. Chartered directors will be expected to undertake continuing professional development (CPD).

Continuing professional development

The IoD define CPD as: 'the systematic maintenance, improvement and broadening of knowledge, experience and skills, and the development of personal qualities helpful in the execution of professional duties throughout a career'. The Institute believes that directors should always be seeking improved performance; and should think of their CPD as a continuing activity, regardless of age or seniority. CPD should be 'owned' and managed by the individual director. The individual must take responsibility for the continuing assessment and satisfaction of his or her own needs. CPD should be systematic; learning objectives should be clear, analysed, applied and evaluated. Development should be professional in that learning must be relevant to a director's responsibilities, and serve board and company needs as well as personal goals.

The IoD believes that CPD is not a specific activity that can be separated from an individual's overall experiences; it is an organic activity, and CPD is a generic description. It should not be seen as an additional task to normal activities, but as an integral part of the way a person manages his or her working life.

IoD policy

IoD policy is that:

- CPD is obligatory for all chartered directors; it is not an optional extra.

- Chartered directors are expected to structure a significant proportion of their learning by means of a personal development plan (PDP).

- Chartered directors must undertake 30 hours CPD a year.

- Chartered directors must keep a record of their CPD activities in a record card.

- Chartered directors are required to provide evidence of their CPD if asked.

Why CPD?

The reputation of the chartered director profession is heavily dependent on the Institute of Directors demonstrating a commitment to maintaining the highest standards of competence among its chartered members. As a chartered director, an individual demonstrates that he or she has a great deal of knowledge and high-quality experience. But this knowledge and experience are relevant only at the time when the qualification was obtained. In a rapidly changing world it is necessary for chartered directors to continue development, and to take advantage of learning opportunities other than formal, off-the-job training.

The benefits of CPD

All IoD members gain from being in membership of a professional institute with a reputation for setting and maintaining high levels of professionalism. In return, they can contribute to the profession through CPD. CPD can also provide some specific personal benefits:

▪ *Improved performance in a director's current role.* Over a working life it is becoming increasingly likely that directors will need retraining and re-educating many times if they are to make a top-quality contribution. The CPD process sharpens awareness of the need for additional knowledge and skills, and encourages directors to plan and achieve the necessary learning.

▪ *Enhanced career prospects.* Being better at a job will obviously improve career prospects directly. In addition, CPD can help directors identify gaps in their present knowledge or skills that may limit the range of opportunities in future. Involvement in CPD will widen their horizons, expose them to different points of view about company direction, and enable them to link their career aims to the future.

▪ *Increased learning capacity.* Prior thought to what might be learnt, and subsequent reflection on what has been learnt and how it might be applied, generally speed up the learning process and enable directors to exploit any activity as a source of learning.

▪ *Greater confidence and self-esteem.* Directors are likely to meet change in a more confident frame of mind than if they had allowed their expertise to stagnate.

▌ *Organizational benefits.* Your company will benefit from the added value of an increasingly effective contribution on its board. Investment in CPD at board level will give a company a competitive edge. Also, a director's personal example may favourably influence the attitudes of fellow directors and senior managers towards their own CPD.

▌ *Public benefits.* CPD gives reassurance to the wider public that all chartered directors are up to date with their knowledge and skills, improves the general level of professionalism across British industry and therefore contributes to economic growth and overall living standards.

Types of professional development recognized by the Institute

CPD is about learning and there are many ways of learning. It is impossible to list all the learning opportunities directors may be able to identify for their own CPD. It is worth emphasizing, however, that much of a director's expertise is learnt through practical experience. CPD is a way of structuring and optimizing the learning opportunities that occur in the director's everyday experience. Part of CPD therefore should be about making more effective use of opportunities for learning on the job.

Types of CPD

The types of activities from which you are likely to obtain a learning outcome are:

1. professional work-based activities, for example:

   – planning and running an in-house training event;*

   – implementing new techniques;

   – learning a new discipline, eg PC skills;

   – making presentations, especially if some research is involved;*

   – coaching or mentoring;*

- committee membership, eg working on the audit committee of the board;*

- visits to other companies;

- attending trade exhibitions and conferences;

2. personal activities outside work:

   - involvement with the activities of the local chamber of commerce, TEC, Business Link or your IoD branch (other than social events);*

   - a range of public duties or voluntary work, eg school governor, magistrate, charity trustee;*

   - membership of and participation on committees or working parties of other professional institutes, trade associations, chambers of commerce, etc;*

   - management of a club or society;*

   - providing assistance to family or friends who run their own businesses;*

   - writing and lecturing;*

3. courses, seminars and conferences:

   - professional education courses leading to relevant recognized qualifications, courses of study, participation in distance learning programmes, the IoD's own short courses and other short courses, whether 'in-house' or by outside providers, on any topic relevant to your development, organized by a competent organization or a suitably qualified individual;*

   - preparation and delivery of papers for conferences, seminars, etc in response to a formal request;*

   - articles and reviews accepted for publication in relation to business, economics, corporate governance, etc;

4. self-directed learning: books, journals, newspapers, documentaries, videos, audio cassettes, eg books published by the IoD, language courses, courses about running a business, law courses, various types of self-development and people skills courses, personal reading plans, reading professional and academic publications (eg *Harvard Business Review* and *Journal of Strategic Planning*).

Activities marked * constitute 'formal' activities. 'Informal' CPD means the other activities listed above and any other form of learning where there is no interaction with other individuals. The IoD is currently developing criteria by which it approves the providers of CPD which would count towards CPD for chartered directors.

The IoD will supply a full pack of advice on how to prepare for CPD.

Code of Professional Conduct

Article 1

A Chartered Director shall exercise leadership, enterprise, and judgement in directing the company so as to achieve its continuing prosperity and act in the best interests of the company as a whole.

Article 2

A Chartered Director shall follow the standards of good practice set out in the Institute's 'Good Practice for Directors – Standards for the Board' and act accordingly and diligently.

Article 3

A Chartered Director shall serve the legitimate interests of the company's shareholders.

Article 4

A Chartered Director shall exercise responsibilities to employees, customers, suppliers and other stakeholders, including the wider community.

Article 5

A Chartered Director shall comply with relevant laws, regulations and Codes of Practice, refrain from anti-competitive practices, and honour obligations and commitments.

Article 6

A Chartered Director shall at all times have a duty to respect the truth and act honestly in his business dealings and in the exercise of all his responsibilities as a director.

Article 7

A Chartered Director shall avoid conflict between his personal interests, or the interests of any associated company or person, and his duties to the company.

Article 8

A Chartered Director shall not make improper use of information acquired as a director or disclose, or allow to be disclosed, information confidential to the company.

Article 9

A Chartered Director shall not recklessly or maliciously injure the professional reputation of another member of the Institute of Directors and not engage in any practice detrimental to the reputation and interests of the Institute or of the profession of director.

Article 10

A Chartered Director shall ensure that he keeps himself abreast of current good practice.

Article 11

A Chartered Director shall set high personal standards by keeping aware of and adhering to this Code, both in the spirit and in the letter, and promoting it to other directors.

Article 12

A Chartered Director shall apply the principles of this Code appropriately when acting as a director of a non-commercial organization.

Appendix 3

The Association of Management Education and Development (AMED)

AMED SERVICES

Strategic directions 1996–2000

AMED is the network for developers, a unique association of individuals committed to developing people and organizations. Within the overall aim of promoting and encouraging management education and development, AMED explores new ideas, shares research and good practice, and develops skills needed for the future, for the personal and professional benefit of people in all communities.

AMED's development values and style distinguish it from other organizations in the international field of management education. We strive to behave in line with our values, modelling these in our activities. We value:

▌ organization and people development as mutually reinforcing;

▌ all individuals in the development process, whatever their role;

▌ clarity, integrity and honesty in theory, principles, research and practice;

▌ feedback from our own and other networks;

▌ change – both practical and attitudinal – as essential to the development process;

▌ the contribution of development to our changing world.

Our strategy, based on our values and our vision for what we wish to become by the year 2000, defines the framework to guide goal-setting and action; it is under continual review and combines what we want to do (our interests and desires), what we could do (opportunities in the environment), what we have to do (our responsibilities) and what we can do (with our competence and resources).
We want to:

▌ develop ourselves as a learning organization;

▌ develop other people and organizations;

▌ build a thriving, active network reaching into Europe and the wider world;

▌ encourage more people to benefit from our network;

▌ become ready for our next phase of development.

We could:

▌ meet changing needs;

▌ enable deeper understanding of development and its impact on the future.

We have to:

▌ fulfil our obligations in law;

▌ meet members' needs.

We can:

▪ encourage curiosity, learning and shared insights;

▪ work on issues that may be difficult;

▪ become even more professional without losing creativity;

▪ innovate.

Guided by members' suggestions, Council sets priority targets from within the following objectives:

▪ to develop ourselves as a learning organization by:

   – making continual opportunities for learning;

   – maximizing learning from all our involvements;

   – promoting diversity of interest, background, need and ability;

▪ to develop other people and organizations by:

   – devising programmes for skill, knowledge and attitude development;

   – working in partnership with others to share skills and experience;

▪ to build a thriving, active network by:

   – enabling and developing local and interest-based networks;

   – identifying and experimenting with new opportunities for networking;

   – focusing interest on different themes and approaches;

   – involving members in decision making and two-way communications;

   – ensuring that individuals and networks experience AMED's benefits;

▌ to encourage more people to benefit from our network by:

    – increasing our membership generally and in targeted sectors;

    – enhancing AMED's profile as the forum for exploring the leading edge;

    – ensuring our activities are accessible to non-members;

    – communicating our successes;

▌ to be ready for our next phase of development by:

    – debating openly and continually reviewing our strategy, approaches and operations;

▌ to meet changing needs by:

    – dealing creatively with issues in our changing world and sustainable development;

▌ to enable deeper understanding of development and its impact on the future by:

    – exploring and communicating what development is and who benefits;

▌ to fulfil our obligations by:

    – working within our constitution, company and charity law;

    – making optimum use of resources;

▌ to meet members' needs by:

    – conducting member surveys and acting on results;

    – taking members' comments and complaints at any time and acting on these;

    – providing professional courses, publications, events and other activities;

▌ to encourage curiosity, learning and shared insights by:

  – stimulating research in key aspects of development;

  – providing opportunities for members to explore research at the leading edge;

▌ to work on issues that may be difficult by:

  – behaving positively in ethics, equality and the environment;

▌ to become even more professional by:

  – aiming for quality and consistency in style, approaches and operations;

  – developing our staff;

▌ to innovate by:

  – developing ideas and setting trends;

  – offering opportunities for experimentation and leading-edge activities.

Appendix 4

The Guidelines of the Commonwealth Association of Corporate Governance (CACG)

We have included the detailed Guidelines of the Commonwealth Association of Corporate Governance as they offer very full advice on director and board roles and responsibilities.

Principle 1 – Leadership

The board should exercise leadership, enterprise, integrity and judgment in directing the corporation so as to achieve continuing prosperity for the corporation and to act in the best interest of the business enterprise in a manner based on transparency, accountability and responsibility.

Every business enterprise should be headed by an effective board, which can both lead and control the corporation, comprising non-executive directors and executive directors. The concept of a unitary board, constituting executive directors with their intimate knowledge of the business and independent non-executive directors who can bring a broader view to the corporation's activities, is the favoured board structure.

Management of the business risk and the exercise of commercial judgment on behalf of the corporation can be positively enhanced by this mutual association and exchange of business experience and knowledge for the benefit of the corporation. The board should, preferably, be balanced as between executive and non-executive directors. The actual proportion will depend on the circumstances and business of each enterprise, and may well be influenced by local law and regulations.

The firm and objective leadership of a chairman, preferably non-executive, who accepts the duties and responsibilities that the post entails, should provide the direction necessary for an effective board.

The board should strive to focus on 'performance' in directing the commercial and economic fortunes of the corporation, and not only concentrate on issues of 'conformance'. The board, under an effective Chairman, must be in a position to ensure a balance between enterprise and control in the direction it gives to the corporation.

The fundamental responsibility of each board is to improve the economic and commercial prosperity of the corporation – regardless of whether it is a private sector or state-owned enterprise.

Each director should be diligent in discharging his or her duties to the corporation, endeavour to regularly attend meetings and must acquire a broad knowledge of the business of the corporation so that they can provide meaningful direction to it. Equally, every director should be aware and conversant with the statutory and regulatory requirements affecting the direction of the corporation and thereby of the society in which it operates.

Principle 2 – Board appointments

The board should ensure that through a managed and effective process board appointments are made that provide a mix of proficient directors, each of whom is able to add value and to bring independent judgment to bear on the decision-making process.

The board should be composed of people of integrity who can bring a blend of knowledge, skills, objectivity, experience and commitment to the board, which should be led by a capable chairman who brings out the best in each director. Crucial to this, is having a proper director selection process to avoid the propensity for 'cronyism' and 'tokenism'. The selection process must be managed by asking what skills are needed on the board to add value to the processes of the board in the context of the business of the corporation. Consequently, the composition of the board should be planned with strategic considerations and objectives of the corporation in mind.

New directors should be familiarised with the corporation's operations, senior management and its business environment and be inducted in terms of their fiduciary duties and responsibilities as well as in respect of the board's expectations. If new directors have no board experience, they should receive training in their unaccustomed responsibility which carries with it significant personal liabilities. The board, as a whole, should be involved in the selection of directors.

Ultimately the shareholders, as owners of the capital of the corporation, have the jurisdiction and discretion to appoint or remove directors but this should always be done through a transparent process at properly constituted meetings.

Principle 3 – Strategy and values

The board should determine the corporation's purpose and values, determine the strategy to achieve its purpose and to implement its values in order to ensure that it survives and thrives, and ensure that procedures and practices are in place that protect the corporation's assets and reputation.

The primary role of the board is to define the purpose of the corporation (that is, its strategic intent and objectives as a business enterprise) and its values (that is, its organisational behaviour and norms to achieve its purpose). Both the purpose and the values should be clear, concise and achievable. The board should be able to exercise objective judgment on the corporate affairs of the business enterprise, independent from management but with sufficient management information to enable a proper and objective assessment to be made by the directors. The board should guide and set the pace for the corporation's current operations and future developments. The board should regularly review and evaluate the present and future strengths, weaknesses and opportunities of and threats to the corporation. Comparisons with competitors, locally and internationally, and best practice are important elements of this process – especially in the new era of the global economy and electronic information.

The board should promote a culture that supports enterprise and innovation, with appropriate short and long term performance-related rewards that are fair and achievable in motivating management and employees effectively and productively. It is imperative that the board seeks to drive the business enterprise proficiently through proper and considered decision-making processes, and recognises entrepreneurial endeavour amongst its management without contravening laws and regulations.

The board, having agreed the purpose and values of the corporation, needs also to identify the corporation's external and internal stakeholders (see Principle 8 for more detail). The board should monitor management's implementation of the corporation's strategic and financial objectives, and the application by management of its policies towards the corporation's shareholders and other stakeholders.

As part of these processes, the board should on a regular basis monitor the corporation to determine that the corporate governance framework in the organisation remains valid and consistent with its strategy and values.

Principle 4 – Company performance

The board should monitor and evaluate the implementation of strategies, policies, management performance criteria and business plans.

The board should define its own levels of materiality, reserving specific powers to itself and delegating other matters with the necessary authority to management. The implementation of these strategies, policies, mutually agreed management performance criteria and business plans must be monitored and evaluated to ensure that they remain relevant and dynamic.

The board must ensure that internal control procedures provide reliable and valid information for this monitoring and evaluation process. These control procedures and systems of reporting must be appropriately resourced and should be reviewed regularly. Internal controls include not only financial matters but also operational and compliance controls and management of business risk associated with the corporation. See Principle 10 for more detail on a formal internal audit process necessary to provide these assurances. The strategies, policies, mutually agreed management performance criteria and business plans of the corporation must be clearly defined and measurable in a manner which is precise and tangible, both to the board and management. Each aspect requires a comprehensive assessment against accurate and relevant information, both financial and non-financial as appropriate, and should be obtained from the corporation's own internal reporting systems as well as external sources so that an informed assessment can be made of all issues facing the board and the corporation in monitoring and evaluating the implementation of these objectives. It is within this context that the corporation's governance structures (see Principle 3 above) should be monitored with constant vigilance to ensure that the business enterprise operates in a manner resulting in enhanced governance.

Principle 5 – Compliance

The board should ensure that the corporation complies with all relevant laws, regulations and codes of best business practice. Directors, at all times, have a duty and responsibility to act honestly and with due diligence and care in their business dealings and to ensure that the corporation epitomises this in all that it undertakes and at every level of the organisation. Each director must comply with the law and associated regulations, and has a responsibility to ensure that the corporation and its employees do likewise.

While the board is accountable to the shareholders of the corporation as the owners of its capital, society expects a corporation to act responsibly in regard to aspects concerning its broader constituency such as the environment, health and safety, employee relations, equal opportunity for all employees, the effect of anti-competitive practices, ethical consumer conduct, etc.

Principle 6 – Communication

The board should ensure that the corporation communicates with shareholders and other stakeholders effectively.

Shareholders and potential investors require access to regular, reliable and comparable information in sufficient detail for them to assess the stewardship of management to enable them to make informed investment decisions. Insufficient or unclear information will affect confidence in the corporation, its board and management and may result in the increase of the cost of capital to the corporation and hamper efficient allocation of resources. Effective communication and disclosure will also help improve public understanding of the structure and objectives of the business enterprise, its corporate policies, and relationships with its shareholders and other stakeholders.

The board should ensure that all communications with shareholders, employees and other relevant stakeholders are timely and accurate. Communication should be understandable and based on the guidelines of openness, with substance prevailing over form. The information provided should be reliable, frank and robust in times of crisis. The communication must enable the reader to evaluate the situation with all the facts in order to take appropriate action.

Obviously, in many circumstances, the requirements for communication with shareholders will be prescribed by statute and/or regulation. Regardless of the effectiveness or otherwise of such regulations, directors nevertheless have a responsibility to ensure that a corporation's communication is in the spirit outlined. This is good corporate citizenship.

The board must recognise that communication will be most effective where it is treated as an on-going pro-active process. The board should ensure that long term strategic decisions are communicated not only to shareholders, but also to the stakeholders whose co-operation will be needed for the long term success of the strategy and thereby the corporation. Directors must not disclose price sensitive confidential information, unless that disclosure has been authorised by the board of the corporation and such disclosure is made public. Neither the board as a whole, nor individual directors must knowingly or recklessly disseminate false or misleading information.

Principle 7 – Accountability to shareholders

The board should serve the legitimate interests of the shareholders of the corporation and account to them fully.

The board should endeavour to ensure that the business enterprise is financially viable and properly managed, so as to protect and enhance the interests of the corporation and its shareholders over time. The board should seek to understand the expectations of shareholders and endeavour to fulfil those expectations when deciding upon the best interests of the corporation. The board should always ensure that all shareholders are treated fairly and provided with appropriate information on an equal basis, irrespective of the significance or otherwise of their interest in the corporation. The board should act in the context that its shareholders, certainly in the case of publicly quoted corporations, are constantly changing. Consequently, decisions should consider the interests of future shareholders as well.

The personal interests of a director, or persons closely associated with the director, must not take precedence over those of the corporation and its shareholders. A director should avoid conflicts of interests. Full and timely disclosure of any conflict, or potential conflict, must be made known to the board. Where an actual or potential conflict does arise, a director should at least refrain from participating in the debate and/or voting on the matter. In the extreme case of continuing material conflict of interest, the director should consider resigning from the board. Any director who is appointed to a board at the instigation of a party with a substantial interest in the corporation, such as a major shareholder or a substantial creditor, should recognise the potential for a conflict of interests and accept that their primary responsibility is to always act in the interests of the corporation.

Directors must not make improper use of information acquired by them in their position as a director. This prohibition applies irrespective of whether or not the director, or any person closely associated with them, would gain directly or indirectly a personal advantage or whether or not the corporation would be harmed – this is as applicable to state-owned enterprises as it is to private sector enterprises. Likewise, a director should not obtain, attempt to obtain, or accept any bribe, secret commission or illegal inducement of any sort and this should be actively discouraged throughout the corporation with appropriate sanction where it is found to have taken place.

In matters of remuneration, the board should set and implement a remuneration policy that creates a reward system to recruit, retain and motivate high quality executive directors.

With reference to the issue of communication with shareholders, and other relevant stakeholders, see Principle 6.

Principle 8 – Relationships with stakeholders

The board should identify the corporation's internal and external stakeholders and agree a policy, or policies, determining how the corporation should relate to them.

Good governance ensures that constituencies with a relevant interest in the corporation's business are taken into account. Corporations do not act independently from the societies in which they operate and, therefore, a business enterprise's corporate actions must be compatible with legitimate societal issues pertinent to its location of activities. The competitiveness and ultimate success of a corporation is dependent on a range of different resource providers including investors, employees, creditors, suppliers, etc.

Hence, the board must take into account stakeholders who may have a direct or indirect interest in the achievement of the economic objectives of the corporation. The board should promote goodwill and a reciprocal relationship with these parties, and be prepared to outline a policy or policies determining and regulating its conduct and relationships with stakeholders identified as having a legitimate interest in the activities of the corporation – whether by way of contractual relationships or as a consequence of the impact of its activities.

The board should recognise that its relationship and communication with interested parties now takes place in a society that demands greater transparency.

It is important to reiterate that while the board remains accountable to its shareholders, it has a responsibility to develop relationships with other relevant stakeholders. This is the modern inclusive approach to directing the fortunes of a business enterprise.

Principle 9 – Balance of powers

The board should ensure that no one person or a block of persons has unfettered power and that there is an appropriate balance of power and authority on the board which is, inter alia, usually reflected by separating the roles of the chief executive officer and Chairman, and by having a balance between executive and non-executive directors.

Effective boards should have a good balance of well-chosen, competent directors who under the Chairman's leadership will shape a strategy for the future of the corporation and direct its interests to ensure profitable performance and sustainable growth over the longer term. Given the importance of the Chairman's role in leading the board, it is recommended to separate this role from that of the chief executive officer. Where the roles of the Chairman and chief executive officer are combined, it is important to ensure that the non-executive directors are of sufficient calibre to bring an independent judgment to bear on issues of strategy, performance, resources and standards of conduct and evaluation of performance. Courage, wisdom and independence should be the hallmark of any non-executive director, so that he or she acts in the best interests of the corporation.

The board should allow every director to play a full and constructive role in its affairs. A director should be prepared and able, where necessary, to express disagreement with colleagues on the board – including the Chairman and chief executive officer.

If a director is in doubt as to whether a proposed course of action is consistent with his or her fiduciary duties and responsibilities, then the course of action should rather not be supported. Independent professional advice should be sought as soon as possible to clarify the position of the director concerned. When a director concludes that he or she is unable to acquiesce in a decision of the board, and all reasonable steps have been taken to resolve the issue, the director should rather accept that resignation or dismissal is a better alternative than acquiescence. Consideration should be given to informing shareholders of instances where a director's resignation or dismissal relates to a policy disagreement of the nature described, as they have the ultimate discretion and jurisdiction in the appointment and dismissal of directors and should be aware of an honest account of any such disagreements between directors.

It should always be remembered that as shareholders are responsible ultimately for electing board members, it is in their interests that the board is properly constituted and not dominated by an individual or group of individuals. However, in practice the board as a whole usually plays a major role in selecting its own members and should accordingly plan for its own continuity and succession.

To remain effective, the board should select, appoint, induct and develop or remove board members as necessary from time to time. Incompetent or unsuitable directors should be removed, taking relevant legal and other matters into consideration. In practice, the Chairman will usually play a lead part in such issues.

Non-executive directors, desirably, should be free from any business or other relationship that could interfere materially with the exercise of their independent judgment (see also Principle 7).

Principle 10 – Internal procedures

The board should regularly review processes and procedures to ensure the effectiveness of its internal systems of control, so that its decision-making capability and the accuracy of its reporting and financial results are maintained at a high level at all times.

It is good practice for boards to create and maintain relevant board committees and to determine their terms of reference, life span, role and function. In doing so, the board should establish, maintain and develop appropriate reporting procedures and proper written mandates or charters for committees such as the executive or management committee which usually oversees the day-to-day implementation of board policy and decisions, the remuneration committee which reviews executive and top management remuneration arrangements, the environmental committee where the corporation's operations warrant such a committee, and the audit committee which reviews amongst other things the internal audit function.

The board should determine a policy for the frequency, purpose, conduct and duration of its meetings and those of its committees. It should also adopt efficient and timely methods for informing and briefing board members prior to meetings. The information needs of the board should be well defined and regularly monitored. Each board member has a responsibility to be satisfied that, objectively, they have been furnished with all the material facts before making a decision.

The board should implement a formal internal audit function. An audit committee should be established to keep under review the scope and effectiveness of the audit (both internal and external) and its relative cost efficiencies. The board should make sure that access between itself and the corporation's internal and external auditors is open and constructive. It should be satisfied that the scope of the audit is adequate, and that management and the internal auditors have co-operated fully. This aspect, while perhaps erring more on the detail than the principle, is critical to assuring the board of the efficacy of a corporation's internal systems of control and financial reporting. However, for all practical purposes, the establishment of an internal audit process may not necessarily be capable of implementation in many of the Commonwealth countries.

As with a number of the principles set out in these Guidelines, it is nonetheless an objective to which all business enterprises should aspire in the fullness of time and development of the corporation.

Principle 11 – Board performance assessment

The board should regularly assess its performance and effectiveness as a whole, and that of the individual directors, including the chief executive officer.

The board should examine regularly the impact of the effectiveness of its directors – collectively and individually. It should set and achieve objectives for continuous improvement in the quality and effectiveness of the board's performance, including performance in a crisis. The board should review regularly the degree to which its objectives are achieved and the quality of the board's decisions.

In order to maximise the efficiency and effectiveness of the board's work, each individual director's performance should be monitored and appraised on an annual basis. Training opportunities for existing and potential directors should be identified and appropriate development undertaken.

The Chairman, whose role is crucial in ensuring that the board is properly led, is responsible primarily for the working of the board and for ensuring that all relevant issues are on the agenda and that all available information on an issue is before the board. The Chairman should also ensure that all directors are suitably enabled and encouraged to play a full role in the board's activities.

Given this pivotal role, the other members of the board should ensure that the Chairman's effectiveness is also appraised annually. In practice, non-executive directors may take a lead role in this appraisal process.

The performance of the chief executive officer, whose principal function is to lead the corporation on a day-to-day basis, should be appraised annually. In practice, the Chairman may take a lead role in this process.

The evaluation of the board should be based on objective and tangible criteria, including the performance of the corporation, accomplishment of long-term strategic objectives and the development of management, etc.

Every director should keep abreast of both practical and theoretical developments in the corporation's direction to ensure that his or her expertise is constantly relevant to the corporation. Continuous and rapid change is now the norm in business, and it is the responsibility of each director to continually and systematically add to their knowledge and expertise in a way that will substantively contribute to the success and prosperity of the business enterprise.

Principle 12 – Management appointments and development

The board should appoint the chief executive officer and at least participate in the appointment of senior management, ensure the motivation and protection of intellectual capital intrinsic to the corporation, ensure that there is adequate training in the corporation for management and employees, and a succession plan for senior management.

One of the board's important responsibilities is the appointment of the chief executive officer. The board should participate, with its chief executive officer, in the appointment of senior management. After all, the board must have confidence in the management to implement its strategies, plans and policies. In this regard, the board owes its duty to the corporation and is thereby accountable to the owners of the corporation's capital (shareholders) for the performance of the business enterprise.

The board must ensure, where necessary, that the corporation's intrinsic intellectual capital is protected by way of trade and employment restraints, copyright, confidentiality undertakings, etc. While this, again, may be considered to extend beyond mere principle to detail, this aspect serves as an example of issues inherent to the success of the corporation. It emphasises the importance with which the board should consider all of the corporation's inherent assets, with particular relevance to its human resources and their development generally in the business enterprise.

Training is an essential part of most businesses today. Where it is needed, the board should ensure not only that it is adequate and relevant but that it will result in the corporation remaining competitive and effective. With the modern emphasis on human resource utilisation, succession planning of senior management is an important board responsibility.

The board should also monitor management and staff morale generally.

Principle 13 – Technology

The board should ensure that technology and systems used in the corporation are adequate to properly run the business and for it to remain a meaningful competitor.

The development of electronic information and technology in the 20th Century has been significant, and the advances in the next millennium are anticipated to be momentous. Competitive advantages may well be derived by a corporation's strategy regarding its use of information technology, and technology generally be it electronic or otherwise, in the efficient utilisation of its assets and processes.

Consequently, a board has the responsibility to ensure that its management information systems, internal controls and technology relevant to the corporation's business are not only updated so that the corporation remains competitive but are of such a nature that they can cope with the planned strategy of the business enterprise in an increasingly competitive world without barriers.

Principle 14 – Risk management

The board must identify key risk areas and key performance indicators of the business enterprise and monitor these factors.

If its strategies and objectives are to have any relevance, the board must understand and fully appreciate the business risk issues and key performance indicators affecting the ability of the corporation to achieve its purpose.

Generating economic profit so as to enhance shareholder value in the long term, by competing effectively, is the primary objective of a corporation and its board. The framework of good corporate governance practices in a corporation must be designed with this objective in mind, while fulfilling broader economic, social and other objectives in the environment and circumstances in which the corporation operates.

These factors – business risk and key performance indicators – should be benchmarked against industry norms and best practice, so that the corporation's performance can be effectively evaluated. Once established, these indicators must be constantly monitored by the board. Management must ensure that they fully and accurately report on them to the satisfaction of the board.

The board, as emphasised throughout, has a critical role to play in ensuring that the business enterprise is directed towards achieving its primary economic objectives of profit and growth. It must, therefore, fully appreciate the key performance indicators of the corporation and respond to key risk areas when it deems it necessary to assure the long-term sustainable development of the corporation.

Principle 15 – Annual review of future solvency

The board must ensure annually that the corporation will continue as a going concern for its next fiscal year.

The intent behind this principle is not that a corporation continues in perpetuity but to have a process in place that will prompt directors to act expeditiously when it is believed that the business may no longer be a going concern.

It is the responsibility of the board, all things being equal at the time the financial statements and annual audit have been completed and reviewed, to satisfy itself that the corporation will continue as a going concern in its next fiscal year. Any conclusion arrived at by the board that the corporation will continue as a going concern should result from the evaluation by the board of objective criteria. The conclusion should be reported in the financial statements for the benefit of the shareholders, but also be communicated as appropriate to the corporation's other relevant stakeholders.

The losses through company failures are felt not only by shareholders – employees lose their jobs, their families lose their livelihood, the consumers lose choice of products, the suppliers lose customers, and the whole economy of a country may possibly suffer as a consequence. The modern approach is to deal with failing corporations pro-actively, rather than reactively. Every corporation saved from failure preserves precious jobs and sustains the economy.

The role of the auditors in ensuring that international standards of accounting and reporting are adhered to by corporations is a fundamental element of this principle.

World-wide the approach is now to rescue and turn around a failing business enterprise, rather than to liquidate and wind it up. It is important, however, for the board to recognise factors and issues – both internally and externally – which may lead to the failure of the corporation and take responsibility for initiating measures likely to sustain its ongoing economic existence. In short, managing the corporation back to health is preferred to liquidation and the choice of resuscitation of a business enterprise should be preferred to bankruptcy.

Appendix 5

Organisation for Economic Co-operation and Development (OECD) Principles of Corporate Governance: An extract

This extract contains a few additional points to those spelt out in the other documents from which we have quoted.

The responsibilities of the board

The corporate governance framework should ensure:

- The strategic guidance of the company,

- The effective monitoring of management by the board, and

- The board's accountability to the company and the shareholders.

Board members should act:

- on a fully informed basis,

- in good faith,

- with due diligence and care, and

- in the best interest of the company and the shareholders.

Where board decisions may affect different shareholder groups differently, the board should treat all shareholders fairly.

The board should ensure compliance with applicable law and take into account the interests of stakeholders.

The board should fulfil certain key functions, including:

▪ Reviewing and guiding corporate strategy, major plans of action, risk policy, annual budgets and business plans; setting performance objectives; monitoring implementation and corporate performance; and overseeing major capital expenditures, acquisitions and divestitures.

▪ Selecting, compensating, monitoring and, when necessary, replacing key executives and overseeing succession planning.

▪ Reviewing key executive and board remuneration, and ensuring a formal and transparent board nomination process.

▪ Monitoring and managing potential conflicts of interest of management, board members and shareholders, including misuse of corporate assets and abuse in related party transactions.

▪ Ensuring the integrity of the corporation's accounting and financial reporting systems, including the independent audit, and that appropriate systems of control are in place, in particular, systems for monitoring risk, financial control, and compliance with the law.

▪ Monitoring the effectiveness of the governance practices under which it operates and making changes as needed.

▪ Overseeing the process of disclosure and communications.

The board should be able to exercise objective judgement on corporate affairs independent, in particular, from management.

Boards should consider assigning a sufficient number of non-executive board members capable of exercising independent judgement to tasks where there is a potential for conflict of interest. Examples of such key responsibilities are financial reporting, nomination and executive and board remuneration.

Board members should devote sufficient time to their responsibilities.

In order to fulfil their responsibilities, board members should have access to accurate, relevant and timely information.

Appendix 6

Investors in People

In April 2000, the Investors in People Standard was updated. The standard's assessment process focuses upon the effectiveness of training and development activities in assisting companies to achieve improved individual, team and overall business performance. There are 12 indicators used in assessment. A review must take place at least once every three years.

To achieve accreditation, companies must ensure that systems and procedures are in place that meet the following principles:

1 Commitment to invest in and develop people to achieve business goals

The indicators are:

- The organisation is committed to supporting the development of its people

- People are encouraged to improve their own and other people's performance

- People believe their contribution to the organisation is recognised

- The organisation is committed to ensuring equality of opportunity in the development of its people

2 Planning how skills, individuals and teams are to be developed to achieve the business goals

The indicators are:

▊ The organisation has a plan with clear aims and objectives that are understood by everyone

▊ The development of people is in line with the organisation's aims and objectives

▊ People understand how they contribute to achieving the organisation's aims and objectives

3 Action to develop and use necessary skills in a well defined and continuing programme directly tied to business objectives

The indicators are:

▊ Managers are effective in supporting the development of people

▊ People learn and develop effectively

4 Evaluating outcomes of training and development for individuals' progress towards goals, the value achieved and future needs

The indicators are:

▊ The development of people improves the performance of the organisation, teams and individuals

▊ People understand the impact of the development of people on the performance of the organisation, teams and individuals

▊ The organisation gets better at developing its people.

Appendix 7

Useful contacts and addresses

SPONSORS

This book was sponsored by AMED and IoD.

Association of Management Education and Development (AMED)
62 Paul Street
London EC2A 4NA
Tel: (020) 7613 4121
Web site: www.amed.management.org

Institute of Directors (IoD)
116 Pall Mall
London SW1Y 5ED
Tel: (020) 7839 1233
Web site: www.iod.co.uk

PROFESSIONAL BODIES AND ASSOCIATIONS

The Association of Management Education and Development (AMED) is an independent, not-for-profit organization. It is one of the leading support organizations for directors and runs a variety of director workshops and development activities.
Association of Management Education and Development
62 Paul Street
London EC2A 4NA
Tel: (020) 7613 4121
Web site: www.amed.management.org

British Chambers of Commerce
22 Carlisle Place
London SW1P 1JA
Tel: (020) 7565 2000
Fax: (020) 7565 2049
e-mail: info@britishchambers.org.uk

The Chartered Institute of Personnel and Development (CIPD) has over 100,000 members and is the professional institute for those involved in the management and development of people. The Institute was awarded chartered status in 2000.
Chartered Institute of Personnel and Development
CIPD House
Camp Road
London SW19 4UX
Tel: (020) 8971 9000
Fax: (020) 8263 3333
Web site: www.cipd.co.uk

The Industrial Society is an independent not-for-profit campaigning body with over 10,000 member organizations from every part of the economy. It has developed Best Practice Direct, a new networking and information service.
The Industrial Society
Peter Runge House
3 Carlton House Terrace
London SW1Y 5DG
Tel: (020) 7479 1000
Web site: www.indsoc.co.uk

The Institute of Directors has over 50,000 members in the UK. Membership of the IoD brings a host of benefits designed to provide directors with the resources and support they need in their day-to-day business dealings. Membership benefits include:

▌ a free business information and advisory service and helpline;

▌ exclusive access to meeting and entertainment facilities in London, Manchester, Edinburgh, Leeds, Nottingham, and Belfast;

▌ reduced rates on IoD conferences and events;

▌ representation to national and local government on key business issues;

▌ free access to 16 UK executive airport lounges whatever class of ticket is held;

▌ free IoD publications (*Director* magazine, *IoD News* and Directors' Guides);

▌ local and national networking opportunities;

▌ wide range of discounted third party benefits.

For information on joining, contact:
Tel: (020) 7766 8888
email: join-iod@iod.co.uk
The Institute started awarding chartered director status to professionally qualified directors in 2000.
Institute of Directors
116 Pall Mall
London SW1Y 5ED
Tel: (020) 7839 1233
Web site: www.iod.co.uk

INFORMATION ON CORPORATE GOVERNANCE

The European Corporate Governance Network (ECGN) Web site contains a collection of international corporate governance codes and principles.
Web site: www.ecgn.ulb.ac.be/ecgn/codes.htm

The International Corporate Governance Network (ICGN) provides a network for the exchange of views and information about corporate governance issues internationally and for the development of corporate governance guidelines. ICGN's 'Statement on Global Corporate Governance Principles' is downloadable from the Web site.
Web site: www.icgn.org/documents/globalcorpgov.htm

The Organization for Economic Cooperation and Development (OECD) in 2000 approved a set of guidelines on the behaviour of multinational companies, which can be viewed on their Web site.
Web site: www.oecd.org/daf/investment/guidelines/mnetext.htm

INFORMATION FOR NEW AND SMALL BUSINESSES

The Department of Trade and Industry publish many documents to support and advise new and existing small businesses. An excellent source of information is *A Guide to Help for Small Business*.
DTI Publications order line
Admail 528
London SW1W 8YT
Tel: 0870 1502 500
Web site: www.dti.gov.uk/publications

INFORMATION FOR NON-EXECUTIVE DIRECTORS

A Web site run by the Institute of Directors and Ernst and Young provides much useful information on all aspects of being a non-executive director.
Web site: www.independentdirector.co.uk

INFORMATION ON QUALITY AND BUSINESS EXCELLENCE

The European Foundation for Quality Management publishes much useful information on quality and business excellence.

European Foundation for Quality Management
Avenue des Plaides 15
1200 Brussels
Belgium
Tel: +32 2 7753511
Fax: +32 2 7753535
Web site: www.efqm.org

INFORMATION ON VENTURE CAPITAL

3i is Europe's leading venture capital company.
3i
91 Waterloo Rd
London SE1 8XP
Tel: (020) 7928 3131
Fax: (020) 7928 0058
Web site: www.3i.com

Business Links (England) are local partnerships that bring together the business support services of the DTI, training and enterprise councils, chambers of commerce, enterprise agencies, local authorities and other local partnerships. There are 80 partnerships. These provide integrated advisory services tailored to the needs of businesses throughout the UK. The Business Link Signpost line can put you in touch with your nearest Business Link and they in turn can inform you of local support networks.
Business Link Signpost line: 0845 756 7765
Web site: www.businesslink.co.uk

In Northern Ireland, the Local Enterprise Development Unit can inform you of local support networks.
Tel: (028) 9049 1031

Advice and support is available from Business Connect (Wales), which will inform you of local support networks.
Tel: 0845 796 9798

Scottish Business Shops provide business information and guidance and will inform you of local support networks.
Tel: 0800 787878

Scottish Enterprise are responsible for advising and helping businesses through Local Enterprise Companies (LECs) and will inform you of local support networks.
Tel: (01463) 234171

Trade Associations represent the interests of special industries or groups of traders and can be valuable sources of advice, information and contacts. The Trade Association forum holds details of Trade Associations.
Web site: taforum.org.uk

BUSINESS NETWORKS FOR WOMEN

For information on business networks for women, see 'Women who network', *Management Today*, September 2000, pp 72–75. The best-known business networks for women are:

E-women
Contact: events@e-women.org

Hightech-women
Contact: www.hightech-women.com

Network
Tel: (01489) 893910

Forum UK
Tel: (020) 8879 7564

TRAINING PROVIDERS

The Institute of Directors in London provides a wide range of training programmes designed specifically to meet the development needs of directors.
Director Development
116 Pall Mall
London SW1Y 5ED
Tel: (020) 7766 8800
Fax: (020) 7766 8765
Web site: www.iod.co.uk
Contact: directordev@iod.co.uk

Distance learning material is also available from the IoD. It provides the same all-round learning needed to direct a modern company successfully from a strategic perspective but in a completely self-contained and flexible programme of modules that directors can complete at their own pace.

Birmingham
The IoD run a company direction programme in Birmingham. For further details contact:
Tel: (020) 7766 8800
Fax: (020) 7766 8765

Durham
The University of Durham Business School run the IoD's company direction programme.
University of Durham Business School
Mill Hill Lane
Durham DH1 3LB
Tel: (0191) 374 2239
Web site: www.durham.ac.uk

Edinburgh
The IoD run a company direction programme in Edinburgh.
IoD Edinburgh
The Royal Scots Club
Admail 3169
30 Abercromby Place
Edinburgh EH3 6ZB
Tel: (0131) 652 3643

Henley
Henley Management College has a Centre for Board Effectiveness. It undertakes research, organizes conferences and provides development programmes associated with improving individual director and board effectiveness.
Centre for Board Effectiveness
Henley Management College
Greenlands
Henley on Thames
Oxfordshire RG9 3AU
Tel: (01491) 571574
Web site: www.henleymc.ac.uk

Leeds

Leeds Business School run an IoD company direction programme in Leeds and Wakefield.
Centre for Director Education
Leeds Business School
Bronte Hall
Beckett Park
Leeds LS6 3QS
Web site: www.lmu.ac.uk

Loughborough

The Management Centre at Loughborough University run an IoD company direction programme.
The Business School
Loughborough University
Loughborough
Leicestershire LE11 3TU
Tel: (01509) 223140
Web site: www.lboro.ac.uk

Salford

The University of Salford run an IoD company direction programme.
University of Salford
Salford M5 4WT
Tel: (0161) 295 5802
Web site: www.salford.ac.uk

Ulster

The Management Institute at the University of Ulster at Jordanstown run an IoD company direction programme.
The University of Ulster at Jordanstown
Shore Road
Newtownabbey
County Antrim
Northern Ireland BT37 0QB
Tel: (028) 9036 5060
Web site: www.ulst.ac.uk

COACHING AND MENTORING

Business in the Community links people with schools and colleges as mentors.
Business in the Community
8 Stratton Street
London W1X 5FD
Tel: (020) 7629 1600

The European Mentoring Centre is involved in researching and disseminating information about mentoring.
The European Mentoring Centre
Burnham House
High Street
Burnham
Bucks SL1 7JZ
Tel: (01628) 661919
Web site: www.mentoringcentre.org

The Institute of Directors offers development and coaching. The coaching process involves a number of steps:

■ Step One: An initial confidential telephone conversation will establish if and how a coach can assist. The process, commitment and costs are explained.

■ Step Two: If appropriate a 1–1½ hour meeting between the coach and client will follow. This will establish the corporate and personal boundaries and the commercial imperatives in the context of the perceived issues and circumstances. A nominal fee of £250 + VAT (2000 price) is charged for this meeting.

■ Step Three: The coaching programme begins. Typically this involves 6 two hour sessions over approximately 3–6 months. At the fourth meeting a progress review establishes if, how and when to continue with a further programme.

Executive Coaching
116 Pall Mall
London SW1Y 5ED
Tel: (020) 7766 8808
Web site: www.iod.co.uk

The National Mentoring Consortium provides support to mentoring activities.
Mentoring Unit
University of East London
Duncan House
High Street
London E15 2JB
Tel: (020) 8590 7722

The National Mentoring Network Business and Technology Centre is a resource centre for community mentoring.
The National Mentoring Network Business and Technology Centre
Green Lane
Patricroft
Eccles M30 0RJ
Tel: (0161) 717 3135

The Prince's Trust provides mentoring for a variety of disadvantaged groups, primarily young adults.
The Prince's Trust
18 Park Square East
London NW1 4LH

BOARD CONSULTANCY

The Institute of Directors Board Consultancy offers services to main, subsidiary and business unit boards and helps them to improve their structure, procedures and performance for enhanced corporate success.
Board Consultancy
116 Pall Mall
London SW1Y 5ED
Tel: (020) 7766 8802
Web site: www.iod.co.uk

NON-EXECUTIVE SEARCH CONSULTANCIES

Many organizations specialize in finding non-executive directors and part-time chairmen. The leading organizations are:

Director Appointments
Boyden International Ltd
24 Queen Anne's Gate
London SW1H 9AA
Tel: (020) 7222 2184
Web site: www.boyden.com

Egon Zehnder acquired PRONED in 1995 and is one of the longest-established organizations specializing in the recruitment of chairmen and non-executive directors.
Web site: www.zehnder.com

Korn Ferry International
Korn Ferry are corporate governance specialists who work closely with clients as a strategic partner in board search.
Web site: www.kornferry.com

There are newer organizations offering their services on the Web. These include:

www.nednet.com
www.nonexecutive.com
www.nonexecdirector.co.uk

References

REFERENCES

Argyris, C (1977) Double loop learning in organisations, *Harvard Business Review*, September–October, pp 115–25

Cadbury, A (1992) *Report on the Committee on the Financial Aspects of Corporate Governance*, Gee, London

Chaitt, R (1993) *The Effective Board of Trustees*, UMP, University of Maryland

Charity Commission (1995) *Responsibilities of Charity Trustees*, Charity Commission, London

Clutterbuck, D (1998) *Learning Alliances: Tapping into talent*, IPD, London

Conyou, M J and Mallin, C (1997) Women in the boardroom: evidence from large UK companies, *Corporate Governance*, (5), July

Cornforth, C and Edwards, C (1999) Board roles in the strategic management of non profit organisations: theory and practice, *Corporate Governance: An international review*, **7** (4), October, pp 346–62

Director, June 2000

DfEE (2000) *Guide to the Law for School Governors*, DfEE, London

Dulewicz, V and Herbert, P (1999) Predicting advancement to senior management from competencies and personality data: a seven year follow up study, *British Journal of Management*, **10**, pp 13–22

Dunne, P (1997) *Running Board Meetings*, Kogan Page, London

Dunne, P (2000) *Directors' Dilemmas: Tales from the frontline*, Kogan Page, London

Eaglesham, J (1998) Door slams on small investors, *Financial Times*, 3 January 1998

Economist, Doing well by doing good, 22 April 2000, pp 183–86

Faulkner, D and Boxer, P (1995) *Consulting*, www.brl.com

Garratt, B (1987) *The Learning Organisation*, Harper Collins, London

Garratt, B (1991) *Learning to Lead*, Harper Collins, London

Garratt, B (1995) *Developing Strategic Thought: Rediscovering the art of direction giving*, Harper Collins, London

Garratt, B (1996) *The Fish Rots from the Head: The crisis in our boardrooms – developing the crucial skills of the competent director*, Harper Collins, London

Garratt, B (2000a) *The Learning Organisation: Developing democracy at work*, Harper Collins, London

Garratt, B (2000b) *Twelve Organisational Capabilities: Valuing people at work*, Harper Collins, London

Greenbury, R (1995) *Directors' Remuneration*, Gee and Co, London

Hampel, R (1998) *Committee on Corporate Governance: Final report*, Gee, London

Hathaway, D (2000) A well connected feel for the company, *Directors and Boards*, Winter, pp 90–92

Hudson, M (1995) *Managing without Profit: The art of managing third sector organizations*, Penguin, London

Hunt, J (2000) Getting to the top is no laughing matter, *Financial Times*, 29 March

Institute of Directors (IoD) (1991) *The Director's Manual*, IoD, London

IoD (1996) *Criteria for NHS Boards*, IoD, London

IoD (1998a) *Good Practice for Board Members: A development guide for Business Link board members*, IoD, London

IoD (1998b) *Sign of the Times*, IoD, London

IoD (1999) *Standards for Good Practice for Boards*, 2nd edn, IoD, London

Institute of Management (IoM) (1995) *Coming on Board*, IoM, London

Janis, I (1982) *Group Think: Psychological studies of policy discussions and fiascos*, Houghton Mifflin, Boston

Kakabadse, A (2000) *The Essence of Leadership*, Thomson, London

Kay, J (1993) *Foundations of Corporate Success*, Oxford University Press, Oxford

Kleiner, A and Roth, G (1997) How to make experience your company's best teacher, *Harvard Business Review*, September–October, pp 172–77

Korn Ferry International (1996) *European Boards of Directors Study*, Korn Ferry International, London

March, L (1999) Recruiting and briefing a new board for an expanding international company, Paper at the 2nd International Corporate Governance Conference at Henley Management College, October

Mescon, M, Albert, M and Khedouri, F (1985) *Management: Individual and organisational effectiveness*, Harper and Row, New York

Mintzberg, H (1975) The manager's job: folklore and fact, *Harvard Business Review*, **52** (4), July, pp 49–61

NHS Executive (1994) *Codes of Conduct and Accountability: Guidance 1994*, NHS Executive, Leeds

PA Consultancy (1994) *Corporate Research*, PA Consultancy, Sundridge Park, Kent

Pierce, C *et al* (1997a) *Developing your Business*, vol 1 and vol 2, Financial Times Knowledge, London

Pierce, C *et al* (1997b) *Directing your Business*, vol 1 and vol 2, Financial Times Knowledge, London

Pierce, C (1998) *Managing Corporate Relations*, Financial Times Management, London

Porter, M E (1980) *Competitive Strategy: Techniques for analysing industries and competitors*, The Free Press, New York

Price Waterhouse (1997) *Converging Cultures: Trends in European corporate governance*, Price Waterhouse, London

Prokesch, S (1997) Unleashing the power of learning: an interview with British Petroleum's John Browne, *Harvard Business Review*, September–October, pp 147–68

Revans, R (1984) *The Sequence of Managerial Achievement*, MCB University Press, Bradford

Rhodes, J and Thame, S (1988) Modelling work through a new thinking profile, *Industrial and commercial Training*, January/February, 1988

Senge, P (1998) The leaders new work building learning organisations, in *The Strategy Process*, ed H Mintzberg *et al*, Prentice Hall, London

Stuart, L (2000) Want to get your own back? Set up a web page then name and shame, *Guardian*, 5 August 2000

Syrett, M and Lammiman, J (1999) The top up principle, *People Management*, 11 March, pp 43–45

Targett, S (2000) Rancher riding high, *Financial Times*, 11 April 2000

Tichy, N and Ulrich, D (1984) The leadership challenge – a call for the transformational leader, *Sloan Management Review*, **26** (1), pp 59–68

Turnbull, R (1999) *Internal Control*, ICAEW, London

Further reading

Blake, A (1999) *Dynamic Directors: Aligning board structure for business success*, Macmillan, London

Dunne, P (1997) *Running Board Meetings*, Kogan Page, London

Dunne, P (2000) *Directors' Dilemmas: Tales from the frontline*, Kogan Page, London

Garratt, B (1995) *Developing Strategic Thought: Rediscovering the art of direction giving*, Harper Collins, London

Garratt, B (1996) *The Fish Rots from the Head: The crisis in our boardrooms – developing the crucial skills of the competent director*, Harper Collins, London

Garratt, B (2000) *The Learning Organisation: Developing democracy at work*, Harper Collins, London

Garratt, B (2000) *Twelve Organisational Capabilities: Valuing people at work*, Harper Collins, London

Hamel, G and Prahalad, C (1994) *Competing for the Future*, Harvard Business School Press, London

Institute of Directors (IoD) (1998) *Assessing Board Effectiveness*, IoD, London

IoD (1999) *Standards for Good Practice for Boards*, IoD, London

IoD (2001) *Guidelines for Directors*, 6th edn, IoD, London

Morton, C (1998) *Beyond World Class,* Macmillan, Basingstoke

Pierce, C *et al* (1997) *Developing your Business,* vol 1 and vol 2, Financial Times Knowledge, London

Pierce, C *et al* (1997) *Directing your Business,* vol 1 and vol 2, Financial Times Knowledge, London

Index